Waters of Zion

Waters of Zion

The Politics of Water in Utah

Edited by Daniel C. McCool

University of Utah Press

Salt Lake City

We dedicate this book to our parents

LIBRARY OF CONGRESS CATALOGING-IN-PUBLICATION DATA

Waters of Zion : the politics of water in Utah / edited by
    Daniel C. McCool.
        p.   cm.
    Includes bibliographical references and index.
    ISBN 0-87480-473-6 (paper)
    1. Water resources development—Utah. 2. Water
resources development—Government policy—Utah.
3. Water rights—Utah.
I. McCool, Daniel, 1950–
HD1694.U8W38   1995
333.91'009792—dc20   95-36947

Contents

ABBREVIATIONS

Bureau	U.S. Bureau of Reclamation
BYU	Brigham Young University
Corps	U.S. Army Corps of Engineers
CRSP	Colorado River Storage Project
CUP	Central Utah Project
CUPCA	Central Utah Project Completion Act (1992)
CUWCD	Central Utah Water Conservancy District
CVP	Central Valley Project (California)
District	Central Utah Water Conservancy District
DWR	Division of Wildlife Resources (Utah)
EIS	environmental impact statement
EPA	U.S. Environmental Protection Agency
GAO	U.S. General Accounting Office
I&D	irrigation and drainage
M&I	municipal and industrial
Metro	Metropolitan Water District of Salt Lake City
NEPA	National Environmental Policy Act
NPCA	National Parks and Conservation Association
NPS	U.S. National Park Service
NWF	National Wildlife Federation
UDPR	Utah Division of Parks and Recreation
UIC	underground injection control
UWRL	Utah Water Research Laboratory (Utah State University)
WRL	Water Research Laboratory (Utah State University)
WSWC	Western States Water Council

FIGURES

TABLES

Preface

In the fall of 1990 I offered a course on the politics of water in Utah. The assignment for the course was to write a book; each student would author a chapter. On the first day of class I had twenty-four students; on the second day I had twelve.

The remaining twelve students were a mix of graduate and undergraduate students. None of them had written a book chapter before, and they appeared to be a bit intimidated by the assignment, but also stimulated by the challenge. I told them a fellow professor had laughed out loud when I described the course goal. "They'll forget about your book the minute they get a grade," he told me. I could see they wanted to prove him wrong.

And so they did. Four years and several revisions later, we have a book. In addition to students in the class, I asked three other water experts—all of them former University of Utah students—to join our project. Thus all of the chapters in this book were written by students or former students at the University of Utah, with the exception of chapters one and nine, which I wrote.

Whenever students publish with their professors, there is always a question as to whether the students actually played an equal role or just assisted the professor. For the chapters in this book, the students did all the research, all the writing, and nearly all of the revisions. I guided them through the process of research, organized the book, and on occasion functioned as project cheerleader, but I did no one's work; all the authors deserve full credit for their own chapters.

Five of the authors were members of the class I taught four years ago: Carrie Ulrich, Roy Ramthun, Ann Pole, Shawn Twitchell, and Ann Wechsler. Kurt Vedder, the author of chapter two, is a recent graduate of the Master of Public Administration program, with a long-standing interest in Utah water history. Terry Holzworth, a graduate of the Executive Master of Public Administration program, has many years of experience in Utah water policy; he collaborated in the writing of chapter three. And Professor Tim Miller, who earned his Ph.D. at the University of Utah, wrote his dissertation on the Central Utah Project and is a recognized expert on water policy. We felt it was important to end the book with an overview of Utah water policy in a national context, and Tim is uniquely qualified for that task.

I should note that the research methodology we followed emphasized the need for objectivity, and I believe the authors did an outstanding job of presenting information in a neutral fashion. However, there are significant political ramifications to this research—we are investigating some of the most far-reaching controversies in Utah history—and not everyone will agree with every author. Furthermore, we realize that, like all westerners, we too have strong personal feelings regarding water policy. Indeed, it was the students' commitment to the wise use of water that gave them the tenacity and energy to stay with this project. Thus a variety of viewpoints are expressed in this book. Each author may or may not agree with the interpretations and conclusions of the others, and the inclusion of an author's chapter in this book does not constitute an endorsement of the interpretations offered by the other authors.

Water is of critical importance to Utah, yet surprisingly, there has never been a book written about the politics of water in the state. This book attempts to fill that gap. One of the most difficult decisions faced by the authors was the choice of topics; there were simply too many fascinating topics to cover them all. Thus, we make no claim to having produced a comprehensive study of the subject; it is our goal to provoke further interest in water policy, in hopes that others will help us research, ponder, and write about one of Utah's most precious resources.

A notable difficulty in writing on a subject that has not been the focus of much scholarly study is the paucity of secondary materials. With so little published research, the authors had to rely almost exclusively on original sources, such as interviews, government documents, and materials provided by interested parties. We also made extensive use of newspaper archives. Our task would have been easier if this book had been preceded by other studies. But of course this gap in the literature gave us an additional incentive to complete this project; we could clearly see that a great deal of research needed to be done on Utah water politics.

The first part of the book, "The Second Driest State," provides a foundation for the book by describing both the political process and the substantive history of water policy in Utah. In the first chapter I provide an overview of both water and water policy. In chapter two Kurt Vedder describes the historical development of water policy in the Salt Lake Valley and then devotes considerable effort to explaining the physical features of the Central Utah Project (the CUP). This helps lay the groundwork for the two chapters in Part II, "Conflict over Priorities: The Central Utah Project." Chapter three, by Carrie L. Ulrich and R. Terry Holzworth, explains how and why the Central Utah Water Conservancy District, the sponsor of the CUP, has changed in recent years. And Roy Ramthun's chapter looks at the conflict surrounding the development of Jordanelle State Park and its potential as a tourist and recreation facility. Both of these chapters deal with elements of the CUP that are of enormous importance, but are not well understood by the general public.

Part III, "Alternative Uses and Sources," begins with Ann Pole's chapter, which describes how cities can increase their water efficiency. In chapter six Shawn Twitchell explains how Utah's groundwater policy has changed over time. Ann Wechsler, in chapter seven, details the increasingly important role of instream flow in state water policy. In the concluding part, Professor Tim Miller places the Utah experience within the larger context of national trends in water policy. And finally, chapter nine provides an up-to-date account of the CUP Completion Act and efforts to implement it.

As a result of this project, I learned a very important lesson: never underestimate your students.

Daniel C. McCool

ACKNOWLEDGMENTS

Any project that spans four years of time generates a lot of thank-you's. First and foremost we express our appreciation to Nana Anderson, former director of the University of Utah Press, and Jeff Grathwohl, the current director. Their patience and encouragement made the difference between success and failure. We also want to thank Zachary Smith, Les Alm, and Paul Culhane, who read earlier versions of the manuscript. At the University of Utah, we owe a debt of gratitude to Professor Dan Hanson, chair of the Political Science Department; Donna Gelfand, Dean of the College of Social and Behavioral Science; and the University Teaching Committee. In addition, our efforts were supported by literally dozens of individuals in state and local government, water agencies, and interest groups; we collectively thank them for their help. And finally, we thank our families, friends, and roommates, who were repeatedly disturbed by incessant typing very late at night.

PART I

The Second Driest State

It is difficult to overstate the importance of water in Utah. This difficulty does not, however, prevent policymakers from routinely doing so: overstatement, hyperbole, and exaggeration are as much a part of the politics of water as the water itself. However, any explanation of water policy, to be meaningful, must include a full array of statistics on usage, supply, price, delivery capacity, and so on. The introductory section of this book explores both ends of the spectrum.

The purpose of the first two chapters is to provide an information base. They present a lot of data and a lot of history. Water policy is complex and has been so for a long time. One cannot understand the current water situation without first understanding this complex history. In addition, one needs a basic knowledge of the resource itself: how much water there is, where it can be found, and what it can be used for.

The first chapter explains how the tendency toward dramatic overstatement has shaped our perspective on water. It also provides an overview of the politics of water, with an emphasis on how water development projects obtain funding. The discussion then turns to "four imperatives" that make contemporary water policy such a challenge.

The second chapter, by Kurt Vedder, provides a historical overview of water development in the Salt Lake Valley. Salt Lake City is unique in many ways. The nearby salt flats are one of the driest places on earth, but the city often experiences dense fog due to the proximity of the Great Salt Lake. The scarce rainfall in the city allows it to be classified as a semiarid region, but the nearby Wasatch Mountains provide a wealth of water. Salt Lake is growing rapidly, though not as quickly as planners predicted just a decade ago. Some of this growth is due to in-migration, but much of it is attributable to the highest birthrate in America. Each new resident in the valley requires a certain amount of water to survive.

Fortunately, Salt Lake's leaders have always been careful to preserve the city's water supply. Most other western cities have been quite haphazard about planning for their water future, but Salt Lake's city leaders have judiciously protected the city's water supply and planned for future growth. Water policymakers have played a powerful role in the city's history.

In arid western cities the water department is often a powerful government entity. For example, the Denver Water Board and southern California's Metropolitan Water District are well known for their ability to wield power and influence. There are several powerful water agencies along the Wasatch Front, including the Salt Lake City Water Department, with a service area including 300,000 people, the Metropolitan Water District of Salt Lake, which is the water development arm of the city, and the Salt Lake County Water Conservancy District, with a service area of over 480,000 people. The Salt Lake Valley is also included in the service area of the Central Utah Water Conservancy District, builder of the Central Utah Project (CUP). In chapter two Kurt Vedder describes the CUP's component parts and explains how they fit together. He also demonstrates how Salt Lake Valley's water agencies have proceeded through a series of eras in their never-ending search for more water.

CHAPTER ONE

Politics, Water, and Utah

Daniel McCool

Mythic Waters

The story of the pioneers diverting water from City Creek always plays a dramatic role in the presentation of Utah history. The water did more than provide sustenance; it symbolically transformed an untamed land into a home. With water flowing across a field of crops, the settlers brought Western civilization to the wilderness and made a future for themselves in an otherwise inhospitable valley. Thus the settlers fulfilled a biblical prophecy and made the desert bloom as the rose. Water became more than just a resource; it was the lifeblood of community, the thread that held together the fabric of society. Water had become the stuff of legend, endowed with mythic powers. Even today the power of water is mythic in our perceptions.

There are many old saws about water in the West: it is more valuable than gold; it flows uphill to money; you can mess with my wife, but not with my water, and on and on. Without a doubt, water is scarce in most of the American West; aridity is a prominent theme in the natural history of the area. Early in the history of the West, however, our image of water was transformed. It was no longer a mere natural resource; rather, it was the key to all success—if we only had enough water, then a robust economy and happy families would naturally follow. This "hydrological determinism" assumes that all aspects of life are determined by the amount of water on hand. Utah Governor Scott Matheson once wrote: "In the eleven contiguous western states, water is the principal limiting factor for future prosperity."[1] A recent brochure produced by the Utah Department of Natural Resources claims, "Water access determines quality of life in all cultures."[2] Of course, if this were true, Oregon and Washington would be fabulously wealthy, and Arizona and Nevada would be economic basket cases.

How did water assume such an exalted position? There are dozens of factors that determine economic prosperity; why was water singled out in the western experience as the most important? I think there are two reasons for this. The first arises from several unique natural features of the American West: enormous expanses of open space, vertical relief in the form of serrated mountains and deep canyons, dramatic variations in temperature and weather, and aridity. Humankind cannot easily change the first three, but water holds the promise of manipulation; it can be stored, diverted, pressurized, directed. We can literally change the course of rivers. Water became the medium by which we could remake the West into a region more suitable for human habitation, one more like the places from whence the immigrants came: the eastern United States and western Europe.

The second reason for water's dominance has to do with politics. Western politicians at the turn of the century wanted federal money to develop water resources, but there were few in Congress who viewed western water development as a significant national priority. Indeed, agricultural development in the West raised the threat of depressing prices for many commodities grown in the East. How could a few stalwart westerners convince an entire nation to spend millions of dollars developing water for the sparsely populated deserts of the West? A mundane claim such as "we want to grow more alfalfa" would never capture the national imagination. So supporters of western water development painted a much more grandiose picture: water development would strengthen the nation, fulfill our collective dream of manifest destiny, and make America even greater.[3]

The debate over the passage of the 1902 reclamation bill is

replete with visions of a society transformed. Supporters claimed that western water development would eliminate the problems of criminality in eastern cities by taking the criminal element out of the cities and turning them into Jeffersonian hardworking yeoman farmers. They claimed that the crowded conditions in eastern cities were the cause of moral decay, which could be alleviated by giving these people irrigated farms in unpopulated areas. And they claimed that dangerous radical political movements such as socialism, anarchy, and organized labor could be disarmed by moving city dwellers out west and giving them a means by which they could raise a crop. This latter argument especially struck a concordant note with many eastern politicians.[4] Thus, in order to get water, and the enormous sums of money it takes to develop it, westerners needed to create a myth—one still with us today.

This myth of water in the western ethos has given rise to a pervasive tendency toward overdramatization; when one speaks about water, hyperbole, and references to the creator are fully expected, often accompanied by an oversimplification of the role water plays in our lives. These activities support the myth of water—a substance so precious that unemotional analysis seems out of place; you are not a "real" westerner unless your temperature rises at the bare mention of the word.

A few examples from the written record regarding the Central Utah Project will help illuminate this point. An early proponent of the CUP predicted that the project would "triple Utah's water supply and solve many of the water problems in the state."[5] When the Colorado River Storage Project Act, which authorized the CUP, was being considered in Congress, project supporters argued that the national security of America was at stake and that the project was "very necessary for the survival of the U.S."[6] Utah Governor George Clyde claimed that the reclamation program would "strengthen our national defense,"[7] and that the CUP was "the key to development of Utah's resources for the next 100 years."[8] Somewhat more modestly, Utah Senator Wallace Bennett argued that the project "holds the key to the future growth" of central Utah.[9]

When the CUP became the target of critics in the 1970s and 1980s, the war of words escalated even further. In its 1973 annual report, the Upper Colorado River Commission claimed the CUP was being "subjected to unmerciful, unreasonable, and unconscionable attacks by ecology and environmental extremists. . . . "[10] CUP proponents described it as "one of the most ambitious water development projects in American History," and as a result, water is "now flowing beautifully" to twelve counties.[11] An "information packet" produced by the Central Utah Water Conservancy District, the local government sponsor for the project, called the enlarged Strawberry Reservoir "the crown jewel and pivotal point of the state water plan."[12] When the project was submitted to a special election in 1985, project supporters warned direly (and fallaciously) that "critical shortages will occur by 1995 without the Bonneville Unit water."[13] Recently the district claimed that failure to build the CUP would "wreak economic havoc" on Utah.[14]

Not to be outdone, opponents of the CUP argued that the project "has resulted in massive ecological trauma and misuse of a vast amount of public funds."[15] Another opponent claimed that future failure of the Jordanelle Dam would result in a catastrophe "as great as Hiroshima."[16]

The latest battle over the project, the 1992 CUP reauthorization act, spawned a whole new generation of hyperbolic statements. In an op-ed piece arguing in favor of the project, the *Deseret News* explained that water "is the one factor that affects everything else. Population, growth, industry, farming, lifestyle, jobs, environment. . . . "[17] When the bill became law, Congressman Wayne Owens claimed, "For forty years, this is the most important legislation passed for Utah."[18]

Despite this transformation of water as resource into water as myth, mundane statistics are essential if we are to understand water policy in Utah.

It is often said that Utah is "running out of water." In fact, the state's watersheds have an annual yield of 8.5 million acre-feet,[19] enough water for 34 million people.[20] Currently the state's total annual water depletions (meaning water that is actually consumed) amount to 4.9 million acre-feet, which is enough for 19.6 million people. And that figure does not include the Central Utah Project, which has yet to deliver appreciable amounts of water.[21]

Clearly there is plenty of water for our homes; but only about 3 percent of the water consumed in Utah is for domestic use, and nearly half of that is for watering lawns. By far the greatest consumer of water is agriculture, which consumes approximately 85 percent of the state's water depletions.[22] The principal irrigated crop grown in the state is hay.[23] A quick look at the statistics on water use reveals a startling fact about Utah's water: nearly all of it is used to grow *grass*—either in the form of hay in farmers' fields or bluegrass in our lawns![24]

In addition to water quantity, we must also consider two other aspects of the state's water. First, many uses of water require that it be diverted, conveyed to a destination, and sometimes stored until needed. The exception to this is instream use, which includes fish and wildlife habitat, aesthetic preservation, watershed protection, and recreation (see chapter seven). Most of the water projects in this state, including the Central Utah Project, are designed to divert, store, and deliver water. In a sense then, the critical issue is how much of the water that we have can we use.

The second aspect of Utah water concerns quality; how clean is it, and can we drink it? Most of the water flowing down from Utah's mountains, which provides much of our drinking water, is of very high quality, and the two-thirds of the public water supply that comes from groundwater is generally high in quality also.[25] The water in Utah rivers, such as the Green and the Jordan, is markedly lower in quality, as is the water in Utah Lake. And, of course, the 20 million acre-feet of water in the Great Salt Lake would have to be desalinated to make it useful.

The state's total population is 1.87 million people; over a million of them live along the Wasatch Front.[26] Much has been made of Utah's status as the "second driest state," a standing that is based on average annual rainfall throughout the state. That average is pulled down by large areas of desert in western Utah; the Wasatch Front is relatively water rich, due to the large snowmelt from the mountains. The Wasatch Range receives approximately 48 inches of precipitation a year, which is comparable to rainfall totals in the midwestern and eastern regions of the nation.[27] Thus cities along the Wasatch Front are in a much better position regarding water supply than many other western municipalities, such as Las Vegas, Santa Barbara, Tucson, and Los Angeles, which have very little local surface water.

Much of the debate over water in Utah has focused on the Central Utah Project, a $3 billion water storage and delivery system begun by the U.S. Bureau of Reclamation (the Bureau) and now being completed by the Central Utah Water Conservancy District (the District). The CUP has five units, but the biggest by far is the Bonneville Unit, which will take water out of the Uinta Basin in northeastern Utah and deliver it to the Great Basin's Wasatch Front. Much of this book is devoted to the CUP because it plays such a prominent role in the continuing debate over Utah water policy. However, there are over a dozen other federal reclamation projects in the state and literally hundreds of water projects sponsored by Utah state government.

An Overview of the Politics of Water

Water development has been an important part of governmental activity since the U.S. Army Corps of Engineers (the Corps) first began clearing snags in 1802. The pace of water development in the West increased dramatically with the passage of the 1902 Reclamation Act, which created the Reclamation Service (by 1924 the Bureau of Reclamation) and established a national policy that utilized water development as a way of populating the West and increasing economic activity.

In the ensuing years both the Corps and the Bureau of Reclamation have built hundreds of projects throughout the West, many of which have created benefits far in excess of their costs. These water development agencies have literally remade the face of the West; entire communities owe their existence to water development programs, and some projects, such as Hoover Dam and Grand Coulee Dam, are stellar examples of successful water development. It can be said with some degree of certainty that most people in the American West depend on water made available through the federal water development program for drinking, recreation, power, or even for their living.

There is no doubt that federally funded water projects serve a lot of people. But many critics argue that the enormous expense of some of these projects cannot be justified.[28] They

argue that many projects are money-losing "pork-barrel" expenditures, meaning that they were selected not according to rational, objective public need, but for the benefit of politicians,
government bureaucrats, and special interests. President Nixon
made this point when he was asked to fund several new water
projects: "Many of these added starts are for projects which
would benefit some particularly interested group but would be
of little value to the people generally. There is too much pork in
this barrel."[29]

The type of policy that often produces pork-barrel government expenditures has two principal characteristics. First, the
benefits of the policy are concentrated where they will provide
the greatest political payoff. Water projects serve this need well
because they can be located in a specific congressional district or
state, and they are very visible; every western politician loves
to cut the ribbon atop a multimillion-dollar dam that brings
jobs and federal money to home-state constituents. Political
pundits often refer to this as "bringing home the bacon." A 1990
Washington Post article noted that "Congress has many sacred
cows, but few are harder to corral than federal water projects."[30]
Proponents of the CUP have used this strategy effectively to
muster political support for the project:

> The water is to be supplied every year at a subsidized cost: For agri-
> culture—the total payment by the farmers is only $16 million on a
> cost of between $800 million and $900 million; for M&I [municipal
> and industrial] water the full allocated cost must be repaid, but we
> have 50 years to pay for it at 3.22%; water for flood control, fish and
> wildlife, recreation and other uses are not reimbursable [do not
> have to be paid back] by the people of Utah. These are paid for by
> the federal government.[31]

Of course the "nonreimbursables," the enormous interest subsidy, and the nearly $1 billion allocated to farmers are not free;
the taxpayers of America must pay for all of these, but this is
overshadowed by the promise of getting a large project from the
government.

The second common element in pork-barrel policy is the
obfuscation of costs; voters may be much less appreciative when
they realize how much they have to pay for the "bacon." Thus,
project sponsors often go to great lengths to hide or disperse the

costs of their projects.[32] One way to do this is to get the federal government to pay for the project; that way the costs are spread out among all the nation's taxpayers. Some of the initial opposition to the Colorado Storage Project Act was based on the claim that it contained "a concealed subsidy from the Nation's taxpayers. . . . "[33]

However, some costs, especially in recent years, must be borne by users and state and local governments. These costs can be hidden by dispersing them among different kinds of taxes.[34] For example, people living in the service area of the Central Utah Water Conservancy District will probably pay for the CUP with their federal taxes, state income tax, state sales tax,[35] monthly water bill, annual property (ad valorum) tax,[36] and electric bill.[37] In the early 1980s, when the District was considering a supplemental repayment contract that would add $335 million to this tax bill, an Interior Department official expressed concern that this additional tax burden was not understood by municipal and industrial (M&I) customers: "I believe we have an obligation—indeed a moral responsibility—to inform M&I consumers about the potential costs they will have to pay. We cannot and should not hide these costs."[38]

In recent years two political developments have made it more difficult to gain government support for pork-barrel water projects. First, environmental opposition to dams made such projects less attractive politically. In the mid-fifties environmentalists stopped Echo Park Dam, which was part of the original Colorado River Storage Project Act. And in the sixties they prevented two dams from being built in the Grand Canyon. By the late seventies, environmental considerations had become an important component of the political equation. As a result, water development may lose more votes than it gains, so water projects have become less attractive to politicians seeking re-election.

A second development concerns federal budgetary problems. In 1980 the national debt stood at $1 trillion; today it is nearly $5 trillion. The budget deficit for fiscal year 1992 was a record-breaking $334 billion (but that didn't stop the Utah delegation from asking Congress to authorize another $1 billion for the CUP). The estimated budget deficit for fiscal year 1996 is

$196 billion. It is getting more difficult to squeeze money out of Washington; if a balanced budget amendment becomes law, federal funds for water development may virtually disappear.

These political developments were reflected in the 1986 Water Resources Development Act, which requires beneficiaries of Corps of Engineers projects to share a significant part of the financial burden. This approach, called cost sharing, has now been applied to the CUP, so people living in central Utah must pay more in taxes to finance the project.

The Central Utah Project and the other Bureau of Reclamation and Corps of Engineers projects in the state have been affected by these national trends in water policy. Over the years, significant changes in water policy have occurred at both the federal and state levels. Changes in water policy in the Salt Lake Valley are discussed by Kurt Vedder in chapter two; recent changes in federal water policy are explained by Tim Miller in chapter eight.

The Four Imperatives of Contemporary Water Policy

Water policy is formulated within a political and a physical context. For many years the political context of water development was relatively simple; when westerners wanted a water project, they got it. Coalitions of business and farming interests worked with the Bureau of Reclamation (or the Corps of Engineers) and their congressional delegation to funnel water development funds to local projects—all paid for by the federal government. These political alliances were often referred to as "iron triangles," and were quite successful in terms of the number of projects built, water diverted and stored, and federal money spent.[39] Usually these projects have consisted of large dams to generate hydropower and store water for irrigated agriculture. To a lesser extent they have provided municipal and industrial water and recreational benefits.

In recent years, however, the traditional iron triangles have lost much of their political clout, primarily due to opposition from environmentalists and tax opponents. This new political reality, combined with the budgetary problems cited earlier, make it more difficult to get new projects through Congress. It has also become much more difficult to obtain presidential approval; Presidents Carter, Reagan, Bush, and Clinton have resisted large-scale water development at federal expense and have insisted on cost-sharing provisos in all major new authorizations. And the Clinton administration has developed an entirely new mission for the Bureau of Reclamation.

This new policy on water development has had a direct impact on Utah. For four years the Utah congressional delegation struggled to enact into law a $924 million reauthorization for the CUP. The law was necessary because all of the previous funding authorized by Congress had already been spent, and the project is still unfinished. The trials and tribulations of the CUP reauthorization are an object lesson in the politics of contemporary water policy and are described at greater length in chapter nine.

The second dimension of water policy is physical; there are only so many dam sites, and there is only so much water. For many years the basic policy of the Bureau of Reclamation and the Corps of Engineers was to solve water problems with structural solutions, which meant the construction of dams, levees, channels, and other water control structures. However, there are limits to how many of these structures can be built. For example, most people agree there are no more dam sites (outside of national parks) suitable for the huge curved-arch dams that were built in the heyday of the construction era.

In recent years federal water policy has shifted more toward nonstructural solutions that rely on better management. Instead of building a flood control dam, for instance, government can simply prohibit construction in a floodplain or refuse to provide subsidized insurance to individuals who insist on building in flood-prone locations. Such an approach is simple, effective, and much cheaper than large-scale construction. Nonstructural solutions may also be more economical; instead of building a large new project to provide additional municipal water supplies, cities can use a combination of regulations, market incentives, and rate hikes to induce greater efficiency in water use. In a sense, the nonstructural water mangement approach is an effort to work within physical limits, rather than trying to change them.[40]

The most dramatic shift in western policy since the passage of the 1902 Reclamation Act occurred in the fall of 1993. Daniel Beard, the commissioner of reclamation appointed by President Clinton, announced a dramatic new policy direction for the agency that would "transform the Bureau of Reclamation from a civil works agency into a preeminent water management agency that is cost effective in serving its customers."[41] The new mission of the Bureau is: "To manage, develop, and protect water and related resources in an environmentally and economically sound manner."[42]

With this political and physical context, water policymakers must consider a vast array of values, preferences, and choices. For purposes of analysis, the authors of this book considered four "imperatives": economic costs and benefits; environmental impact; questions of equity and justice, and social and cultural impact. Most contemporary conflicts over water include all four of these issues.

Economic Costs and Benefits

Economic benefits play an important role in the effort to generate political support for a project. Federal water projects are required to produce benefits that are equal to or exceed costs as measured by the formal process of benefit-cost analysis. When benefit-cost analysis was first required in the 1930s, policy reformers, especially economists, viewed it as a major improvement. However, there is no requirement that these analyses be performed by an outside, neutral party. Instead, the Bureau and the Corps analyze the costs and benefits of their own projects, and sometimes they skew the analysis in order to justify projects that are politically popular but of questionable economic value.[43]

Critics charge that the Bureau's standardized method of analysis overestimates benefits and underestimates costs. For example, their analyses do not include the interest subsidy as a cost; if they did, many recent projects would not have a positive benefit-cost ratio. The Bureau claims that 84 percent of its project costs are returned to the treasury, but if the interest subsidy is included, this figure drops to between 10 and 14 percent.[44] According to the Bureau's own analysis, the interest subsidy averaged over $500 million a year in the 1980s.[45] In the case of the CUP, the interest subsidy is significant; the municipal and industrial portion of the project pays only 3.22 percent interest, and the irrigation component pays no interest at all. Over the period of the loan (fifty years), the revenue lost to the federal treasury will amount to many millions of dollars. Even project supporters admit that using a realistic interest rate (for example, 7.875 percent) would produce a negative benefit-cost ratio.[46]

Regardless of the disagreements over how benefit-cost analysis should be done, the CUP will have a substantial economic impact. The District claims the Bonneville Unit will create ten-thousand person-years of employment and "assure continued economic growth to Utah."[47] Project opponents admit the CUP will bring jobs and money to Utah, but they counter that we must consider "opportunity costs," meaning all other economic opportunities that are forfeited because the revenue is tied up in the CUP. The real economic question is: Are there other, more productive and profitable ways to spend $3 billion? Some argue that the greatest economic efficiency would be realized by reducing taxes by $3 billion. Then individuals and private entrepreneurs could spend the money in a way that maximized their benefits. Basically, they argue that the free market is inherently more efficient, and thus will produce more overall wealth, than large, government-subsidized programs.

In the final analysis, few elements of the economic debate over the CUP and other water projects can be isolated from the other three imperatives; economic return is important, but it must be considered in light of other societal goals.

Environmental Impact

As late as the mid-1950s, water projects were built without consideration of environmental impact. Today it is nearly impossible to get a project through Congress if it creates significant environmental degradation. Many Utahns are quite concerned about their environment. Fifty percent of the respondents in a recent poll agreed with the statement, "We must protect the environment even if it means jobs in our community are lost because of it." And 61 percent agreed that we should slow the rate of population growth to protect the environment.[48]

There are two ways to prevent or minimize environmental damage from government-built water projects: stop the project altogether or incorporate mitigation measures into project design. In recent years environmentalists have been successful in stopping some water projects because of their impact on the environment, but a more common strategy is to insist that mitigation measures be included in projects.[49]

Initially, environmentalists argued on the basis of aesthetics, but they soon realized that economic arguments generated greater political impact. Economic analyses by environmental groups exposed inefficiencies in projects and demonstrated that some projects were pure pork barrel. This in turn generated a lot of media coverage, which disrupted the quiet, behind-the-scenes operations of the water iron triangle. In the past, water policy decisions were made behind closed doors by a small group of people who gained a direct advantage from using public funds to develop water resources. Now water policy decisions are among the most visible and contentious issues on the political agenda. For example, the 1994 draft environmental impact statement for Glen Canyon Dam generated over thirty-three thousand comments.[50]

This increased level of conflict and visibility has not stopped water development altogether. Rather, environmental protection must be considered along with traditional goals of water policy. In some cases this can be accomplished by including mitigation and protection measures in the design of a new project, as when during the formulation of the CUP reauthorization bill, environmental groups were brought into the process. Environmental mitigation became a significant part of the bill, and eventually forty environmental and outdoor sports groups officially sanctioned the reauthorization of the project.

Questions of Equity and Justice

Formulating water policy would be a simple matter if decisions could be made solely on the basis of economic data, but decisions regarding water and funding must consider our perceptions of what is just and fair. Much of the discussion regard-

ing equity and justice involves two issues: claims that promises
have been broken and conflict over who should pay.

In regard to broken promises, one of the most vexing problems concerns the Northern Ute Tribe, whose reservation lies
in the Uinta Basin.[51] The water supply for the CUP is heavily
dependent on water from the Uintah and Ouray Reservation,
the homeland of the Northern Utes. When the Bonneville Unit
was still just a gleam in the water developers' eyes, an early
planning document made it quite clear that the project could not
go forward without an agreement with the Northern Ute Tribe:

> The clarification of Indian and non-Indian water rights is prerequi-
> site to final planning for both local development of water resources
> and for exportation of water from Colorado River tributaries to the
> Bonneville Basin. An agreement between CUP and the Ute Indians
> limiting the total acreage of Indian-owned and Indian water rights
> land is a must for successful operation.[52]

In 1965 the tribe signed an agreement relinquishing much of its
water to the CUP in exchange for a large water project, but the
Bureau never built the Indian project.[53] It did, however, construct Upper Stillwater Dam, which diverts water from the
reservation to Strawberry Reservoir for use by non-Indians. In
1989 the tribe declared the 1965 agreement void because "the
non-Indian parties breached their obligations to the Ute Indian
Tribe."[54] This left the CUP in an untenable legal position. The
tribe, the District, and federal and state officials have negotiated
a settlement and a compact that compensates the Utes for losses
resulting from the government's failure to build the Ute Indian
portion of the CUP. However, at this writing the tribe has not
ratified the compact, so that part of the project is still in legal
limbo.[55]

Another element in the debate over fairness concerns allega-
tions that the federal government, by authorizing the CUP,
made an irrevocable commitment to the people of Utah. The
CUP was authorized in 1956 as part of the Colorado River
Storage Project,[56] but funding for the project has been difficult to
obtain, especially in recent years, due to political opposition to
the project. When President Jimmy Carter placed the Bonneville
Unit of the CUP on his famous "hit list" of water projects to be
terminated, proponents of the project argued that such a termi-

nation would be "an abrogation of moral commitments to Utah people developed over a period of many years."[57] In a recent scoping report for the Uinta Basin Replacement Project, one of the comments from a Uinta Basin resident made a similar point: "We feel we have been short changed in this CUP deal. This dam was promised and we feel the Government should live up to their end of the bargain. Don't let the environmentalists and Indians beat us out of this."[58]

It is important to understand, however, that all federal expenditures go through a two-step process. First, funding must be authorized, meaning Congress gives its consent to a particular program or project and will permit a specific amount of money to be allocated to that project. The second step, the appropriation process, is an annual procedure made through an entirely different set of committees and subcommittees; appropriation bills obligate a specific amount of money that can be spent that fiscal year. In regard to water projects, it is not uncommon for Congress to authorize projects but never spend any actual money on them.[59] This is how the procedure works, but to someone who has waited thirty years for a water project, it undoubtedly seems to be an unfair process.

Equity questions also involve debate over paying a "fair share." All big water projects are a reallocation of wealth, usually from a large group of taxpayers to a specific group of beneficiaries. One of the most persistent fair-share questions regarding the CUP involves the relative payback obligations of irrigators, urban water users, and power customers. Western irrigation requires enormous amounts of water and expensive storage and delivery systems. Yet farmers pay only a small fraction of the actual cost of the water they receive. The Bureau of Reclamation usually solves this problem by combining irrigation projects with the delivery of municipal and industrial water and the production of hydropower; it then charges more for electric power and M&I water in order to subsidize the costs of the irrigation component. The federal treasury covers any remaining costs.   Generally, this results in a significant subsidy of rural areas at the expense of primarily urban areas.[60] According to some estimates, the CUP's irrigation component, if fully developed, would deliver water at a cost of over $6,000 per acre-foot, with a capital investment of $24,000 (assuming 4 acre-feet of water for each acre), yet farmers would pay back only $9.40 per acre.[61] Critics question whether it is fair to impose these costs on urbanites and public power customers. Defenders of the project argue that increased agricultural development is good for the state as a whole, because it generates increased economic activity in the state: "The gross income for farm families will be increased by about $25 million and an estimated $45 to $50 million will be invested by farmers as project water becomes available."[62] What is "fair" is clearly influenced by who is paying for, and who is receiving, the benefits of water development.

Social and Cultural Impacts

Much of the debate over issues of justice and equity is, in a more general sense, a debate over the long-term impact that water development has on society and culture. The Northern Utes see a close connection between water and the continued survival of their culture, and the urban-rural question also has significant long-term social implications.

One interesting example of the impact of water on society concerns "water ranching," which refers to the practice of buying irrigated farmland, retiring it, and transferring the water to municipalities.[63] As a practical matter, water ranching is eminently sensible; it is often the cheapest way to acquire new water supplies for growing cities. The state water plan assumes that 110,00 acres of cropland in Utah will be converted to urban uses by the year 2010. This will free enough agricultural water to provide for the needs of approximately 2.2 million people.[64] In Salt Lake County about half of all water withdrawals are for agriculture; if just half of this land were retired, it would free approximately 140,000 acre-feet. That is twice the amount of M&I water the CUP will deliver to Salt Lake County and City and enough water for about 560,000 people.[65]

But there is another side to this story. Water ranching can devastate rural economies by removing productive land from the tax base. Also, many farmers view farming as a way of life, not just an occupation—an argument that often produces the response: "That's fine, but don't ask us urbanites to pay for it." But the situation is more complicated than that. If we reduce agricultural activity in favor of municipal water usage, many rural people may be forced to leave the countryside and move to the city. This could exacerbate a wide variety of urban problems, problems that are often quite costly to solve. It may be that society needs a balance between rural and urban economic activity. These are difficult questions, beyond the reach of conventional benefit-cost analysis.

The theory of hydrological determinism would put all aspects of society at the mercy of the water supply. Although reality is much more complicated than that, there is no doubt that water policy can be an important tool in shaping society and nurturing, or decimating, cultures.

150 Years of Utah Water Policy

In the following chapters, the authors describe a complex array of events, behaviors, and outcomes. Each of them is unique in some way, but each is also part of a larger process of deciding what to do with our water. If we step back and view Utah water policy from that day 150 years ago when the first intrepid Mormon settlers diverted City Creek, to the most recent efforts to implement the CUP Completion Act, we can discern five characteristic themes.

First, it is apparent that Utah's water policy has moved through a series of stages or eras, and this process continues today. These eras are laid out explicitly in Kurt Vedder's chapter, but they are implied in the other chapters that explore new ways to use water and new concepts in governing water. The reader may want to speculate: what should we call the current era? What will be the next era?

Second, water policy has been the focus of enormous energy and innovation. Engineers have demonstrated tremendous creativity in building complex physical structures to harness the flow of water, and politicians have displayed extraordinary ingenuity in developing political, legal, and bureaucratic mechanisms to plan, fund, and implement water resources programs.

And perhaps the greatest demonstration of innovation occurs when we make a transition from one era to the next; at each of these junctures leaders have emerged to lead the state into the future.

A third theme in Utah water policy is the relationship between the amount of water and the number of people in the state. As population has increased, so too has the relative scarcity of water.[66] This has often provoked bitter conflicts, but ultimately has led to the next stage of policy, as old institutions and old ways of thinking has given rise to new concepts and approaches.

A fourth theme in Utah water policy is that everything must be taken in context. It is interesting to travel to small towns in remote sections of Utah and hear people talking about water policy decisions that are the result of political events thousands of miles away. Even in the past, when the water iron triangle supposedly operated as an autonomous fiefdom, larger trends in politics were influencing Utah water; East Coast members of Congress voted for the 1902 reclamation bill so they could gain additional votes for river and harbor projects in their districts: a Supreme Court decision in 1908 affecting the remote Fort Belknap Reservation in Montana made the Ute Indians big players in the CUP sixty years later; the 1956 Colorado River Storage Project Act was passed, in part, due to Cold War fears about a Soviet invasion. In recent years the larger political, economic and social context has become even more important: the federal budget deficit; world agricultural markets; the selection of Bruce Babbitt as secretary of the interior; and global warming. We may not want to admit it, but today foreign tourists may have more influence than local ranchers in deciding how to use our water.[67]

A final theme concerns what we might call a "water mindset." Public officials, interest groups, and the public often make assumptions about water that, over time, solidify to become a kind of water gospel, and it is politically risky for anyone to even question their veracity. There are at least three major elements in the Utah water mindset. First, we all "know" we are running out of water. This has led to a singular devotion to supply solutions, usually to the exclusion of demand solutions;

instead of using water more efficiently or more wisely, we assume we need a greater quantity of water.

A second element in the Utah water mindset is the "California threat." The water policy establishment in Utah has always passionately held that, if we do not use our Colorado River water, "California will get it." This belief is widespread and fervent, despite the fact that such a water grab is clearly and unambiguously illegal. However, the California threat provided an excellent rationalization for building the CUP.[68]

Another element in the mindset is that nearly everyone in Utah has believed, for at least four decades, that the CUP is the best way—indeed the only way—to solve our water problems. The two major newspapers in the Salt Lake area, every senator and representative from Utah, every Utah governor, and the region's many water organizations have relentlessly campaigned for the CUP; until the mid-1980s, the citizens of Utah had never heard an opposing argument. Indeed, when a draft report critical of the CUP was issued by the Utah Water Research Laboratory in 1983,[69] the general manager of the Central Utah Water Conservancy District responded with a threat: "If it [the report] is published without being extensively modified, the District will pursue every possible action to discredit this report, its authors and any associated studies."[70] One of the authors of the report, Professor Jay Bagley, replied that "university researchers' findings cannot be suppressed or manipulated by threat or intimidation."[71] But in fact, the response of the Utah water establishment to the report made it quite clear that criticism is risky.

In a rational policy-making process, water planners would determine how much additional water was needed, compare a variety of different methods for obtaining that water, and then select the method that was the most cost efficient. However, this was not done before the state's water establishment devoted itself wholeheartedly to the CUP. If such a comparison were to be done, it is quite possible that a number of other options would be significantly cheaper than CUP, including: increased groundwater usage; dual water systems; water ranching; water-use efficiency measures; water reuse, and free-market pricing of water. However, the Utah water mindset did not permit such an objective cost comparison when the CUP was being planned.

In 1973 the members of the Upper Colorado River Commission, in a statement with a militancy uncharacteristic of a taxpayer-funded public agency, declared they would use "any measures necessary" to expedite construction of the CUP.[72] Although they may not have been entirely aware of it, they were adamantly resisting the advent of a new era in water policy. Today the attitude of many public water officials is quite different. With a much larger and more varied population and a fundamentally different political situation at the national level, policymakers are searching for innovative ways to meet our water needs. The main goals of this book are to describe both the old and new approaches to water policy and to help explain how the transformation from one to the other has taken place.

Notes

1. Scott Matheson and James Kee, *Out of Balance* (Salt Lake City: Peregrine Smith, 1986), p. 161.

2. "Utah Water Summit." November 15, 1994. Sponsored by the Utah Department of Natural Resources.

3. The motto of the day was that the reclamation act would "put the landless man on the manless land."

4. For a more detailed description of this process, see Daniel McCool, *Command of the Waters: Iron Triangles, Federal Water Development, and Indian Water,* chapter 2 (Berkeley: University of California Press, 1987); reissued in 1994 in paperback by the University of Arizona.

5. Rene Ballard, "The Salt Lake Metropolitan Water District" (Salt Lake City: Institute of Government, University of Utah, December 1948), p. 15.

6. "Our National Defense Demands the Upper Colorado River Storage Project" (Grand Junction, Colo.: Upper Colorado River Grass Roots, Inc., [ca. 1955]). This flyer claimed that the building of dams on the Colorado would "enable us to disperse our new vital industries behind our own 'Ural' mountains."

7. *Congressional Record,* 87th Cong., 1st sess., June 28, 1961.

8. Central Utah Project, "Initial Phase, Definite Plan Report," August 1964, p. 14. Governor Clyde was a former director of the Utah Water and Power Board.

9. *Congressional Record,* 87th Cong., 1st sess., "Speeches of Hon. Wallace F. Bennett, June 28 and 29, 1961." It is ironic that Bennett could wholeheartedly support this massive government project but oppose public power lines as an example of "creeping socialism" that must be opposed to "preserve Americanism." (*Murray Eagle,* June 1, 1961).

10. "Twenty-Fifth Annual Report" (Salt Lake City: Upper Colorado River Commission, September 30, 1973), p. 25.

11. Central Utah Water Conservancy District, "Water . . . Brought to You by the Central Utah Project" (Salt Lake City: published as a newspaper supplement, November 1990.) In reality the CUP had not delivered any water to the Great Basin.

12. Central Utah Project, "Information packet," September 1989.

13. Central Utah Water Conservancy District, flyer produced for use in the 1985 campaign, n.d. This flyer concludes with the statement that some have raised objections to the project, "but none of these concerns are valid."

14. Central Utah Water Conservancy District, "Jordanelle Dam," flyer, n.d., ca. 1994.

15. "The Central Utah Project: A Critical Review of Important Problems," published by a coalition of ten groups, September 1989.

16. Letter from Jackson Howard of Provo, Utah, to Congressman Howard Nielson, April 4, 1989.

17. *Deseret News,* January 17, 1990, p. A-8. This statement could also be made for air, land, government policy, the weather, taxes, sex, etc.

18. *Deseret News,* October 31, 1992, p. A-1.

19. State Water Plan Coordinating Committee, "State Water Plan" (draft), January 1990, sec. 2, p. 3. One acre-foot equals 325,851 gallons.

20. This assumes that one acre-foot per year is enough water for a family of four. The water literature uses a family of either four or five as the commonly accepted standard. If the latter figure is used, the state's water supply is sufficient for 42.5 million people.

21. "State Water Plan," sec. 2, p. 3. The Central Utah Project's Bonneville Unit was originally planned to deliver 294,000 acre-feet of water. As the project is scaled back, however, the total diversion will be reduced.

22. "State Water Plan," sec. 9, p. 1, places this figure at 80 percent, but most other sources indicate that it is higher than that. Data supplied by the Utah Division of Water Resources indicate that "agriculture and irrigation" use 87.3 percent, "public and domestic" uses account for 9.2 percent, and "commercial and industrial" use consumes the remaining 3.5 percent. However, a 1994 brochure produced by the division, titled "Water in Utah," states that only 70 percent of the state's developed water is used by agriculture.

23. Although hay consumes the most water, it only produces 7.5 percent of the state's farm receipts. Considering that all forms of agriculture in Utah generate only 1.5 percent of the gross state product, it is apparent that hay is not a critical element in the state's economy. Utah Office of Planning and Budget, "Annual Economic Report to the Governor," 1994, pp. 66, 121.

24. David Ovard of the Salt Lake County Water Conservancy District recently noted that "all new development of sources [of water for Salt Lake County] will be to provide for outside watering." Comments made at the annual conference of the American Water Resources Association, Utah Section, Salt Lake City, May 13, 1993. In other words, we are building the CUP to water our lawns.

25. State of Utah Water Quality Assessment for 1992 [Section 305(b) Report].

26. Due to in-migration and the highest birthrate in the nation, the state's population is increasing rapidly. Utah Office of Planning and Budget, *Annual Economic Report to the Governor,* 1994, pp. 73–77.

27. It is somewhat ironic that the second-driest-state figure is often used to

justify building the CUP, which will deliver water primarily to the areas of the state with the most precipitation.

28. For example, one recent study investigated eighteen Bureau irrigation projects, and found that costs exceeded benefits on eleven of them. See Richard Wahl, *Markets for Federal Water: Subsidies, Property Rights, and the Bureau of Reclamation* (Washington, D.C.: Resources for the Future/Johns Hopkins University Press, 1989). Also see President Jimmy Carter's assessment of water projects, which resulted in his famous "hit list," *Weekly Compilation of Presidential Documents: Jimmy Carter* (Washington, D.C.: U.S. GPO) vol. 13, 1977: pp. 234, 315–16, 403–4, 557–59.

29. *Public Papers of the Presidents: Richard Nixon* (Washington D.C.: U.S. GPO, 1970) pp. 824–25.

30. *Washington Post*, October 17, 1990, A-10.

31. CUP "Information Packet," p. 32.

32. Jon R. Miller, "On the Economics of Western Local Water Finance: The Central Utah Experience," *Land Economics* 69 (August 1993): 299–303. Also see B. Delworth Gardner, "Water Pricing and Rent Seeking in California Agriculture." In *Water Rights: Scarce Resource Allocation, Bureaucracy, and the Environment,* ed. by Terry Anderson (Cambridge, Mass.: Ballinger Press, 1983).

33. Committee on Interior and Insular Affairs, U.S. House of Representatives, "Colorado River Storage Project and Participating Projects," Minority Report, June 9, 1954, p. 31. This report calls the CUP "the most infeasible of all" the projects in the bill. The committee voted in favor of the bill by a one-vote margin.

34. They can also be hidden by transferring them from one project purpose to another. See Jon R. Miller, "The Political Economy of Western Water Finance: Cost Allocation and the Bonneville Unit of the Central Utah Project," *American Journal of Agricultural Economics* (May 1987): 303–10.

35. In 1994 the state legislature passed SB 212, which earmarks 1/8 of one cent of the general sales tax to water development. The CUWCD will probably receive some of this money.

36. A water conservancy district is allowed by law to levy four different kinds of property taxes. See J. M. Bagley, et al., "Impediments to Effective Interactions Between Multipurpose Water Districts and Other Governmental Institutions in Urbanizing Areas," Utah Water Research Laboratory, Utah State University, June 1983.

37. It is doubtful that anyone in these twelve counties knows how much this project will really cost them in taxes. If all the taxes for the CUP were paid annually in one lump sum, like property taxes, the level of public support for the project would undoubtedly diminish.

38. Guy Martin, (assistant secretary for land and water resources), "Comments on the Proposed Bonneville Unit, CUP Supplemental Repayment Contract, Memorandum to Commissioner," Water and Power Resources Service, January 18, 1981.

39. Daniel McCool, *Command of the Waters: Iron Triangles, Federal Water Development, and Indian Water* (Berkeley: University of California Press, 1987); reissued in 1994 (Tucson: University of Arizona Press). See also Robert Gottlieb, *A Life of Its Own: The Politics and Power of Water* (New York: Harcourt Brace Jovanovich, 1988). For a more sensationalized account, see Marc Reisner, *Cadillac Desert* (New York: Viking Press, 1986).

40. The basic difference between "water development" and "water management" is that the former alters the behavior of water whereas the latter alters the behavior of people in relation to water.

41. U.S. Department of the Interior, "Bureau of Reclamation Announces Reforms: Meets Challenge of the National Performance Review," news release, November 1, 1993.

42. Daniel P. Beard (commissioner), "Blueprint for Reform: The Commissioner's Plan for Reinventing Reclamation," U.S. Bureau of Reclamation, November 1, 1993.

43. For a review of the scholarly literature regarding the abuses of benefit-cost analysis, see McCool, *Command of the Waters*, pp. 96–97.

44. Wahl, *Markets for Federal Water*, p. 42.

45. U.S. Congress, House, Hearings before the Subcommittee on Energy and Natural Resources, Committee on Appropriations, 100th Congress, 2d sess., 1988, "Energy and Water Appropriations for 1989," p. 64.

46. Central Utah Project State Review Team, "State Review of the Bonneville Unit, Central Utah Project," draft, Utah Department of Natural Resources, September 1984, pp. 36–37.

47. Central Utah Water Conservancy District, "Economic Impact, Bonneville Unit of the Central Utah Project," brochure, Orem, n.d.

48. University of Utah Survey Research Center, "Utah Consumer Survey, January 1994 Report" (Salt Lake City), p. 49.

49. See Tim Palmer, *Endangered Rivers and the Conservation Movement*, (Berkeley: University of California Press, 1986).

50. Colorado River Studies Office, "Operation of Glen Canyon Dam," draft environmental impact statement, public comments analysis report (August 1994), p. 1.

51. See Richard White and Ed Marston, "How the Ute Tribe Lost Its Water," *High Country News*, March 30, 1987, p. 11; Daniel McCool, "The Northern Utes' Long Water Ordeal," *High Country News*, July 15, 1991, pp. 8–9.

52. "Duchesne River Land and Water Resource Review," April 1962, p. 5. On file, Bureau of Reclamation, Bennett Federal Office Building, Salt Lake City.

53. The Bureau did not finance the Ute Indian project, but it did manage to find the funds to build a bowling alley in Duchesne, just off the reservation.

54. Tribal Resolution no. 89-175, adopted September 20, 1989.

55. The Ute Indian Water Settlement is part of the CUP reauthorization act. The accompanying Ute Indian Water Compact between the tribe and the state cannot be implemented until it is approved by both the state legislature and a tribal referendum. Approval by the state legislature is expected; approval in a tribal referendum is in doubt. See Daniel McCool, "Utah and the Ute Tribe are at War," *High Country News*, June 17, 1994, p. 12.

56. 70 Stat. 105, enacted April 11, 1956.

57. State of Utah and the Central Utah Water Conservancy District, "Compilation of Supplementary Documents in Support of Continued Funding for the Bonneville Unit of the Central Utah Project," filed with the special panel assembled to review the Bonneville Unit, Mar. 23, 1977, chapter titled "Alternative Plans," p. 15.

58. Uinta Basin Replacement Project, "URBP Scoping Report," March 1994, prepared for the Central Utah Water Conservancy District.

59. This is because it costs nothing for a legislator to authorize a project, but he/she can still claim credit for such an authorization. Thus, it is an easy way to bring home the bacon. When the 1986 Water Resources Development Act was passed, it deauthorized over three hundred corps projects that had never received any funding.

60. The hydropower facilities planned for the CUP have been eliminated from the project due to a lack of market customers for the power. The costs that would have been absorbed by these hydropower facilities now have to be paid by other project purposes—primarily M&I and other hydropower facilities in the Upper Basin regional power area.

61. U.S. Senate, "Miscellaneous Water Resource Measures, June 9, 1988, Testimony of Senator Bill Bradley," hearings before the Subcommittee on Water and Power, Committee on Energy and Natural Resources, p. 2.

62. Central Utah Water Conservancy District, "The Central Utah Project," brochure, Orem, Utah, n.d.

63. This is already occurring in Utah on a small scale. See Ray Jay Davis, "Utah Water Rights Transfer Law," *Arizona Law Review* 31 (1989): 841–64.

64. "State Water Plan," sec. 10, p. 2. The figure of 2.2 million assumes an average application of 5 acre-feet per acre, converted to domestic use where one acre-foot is sufficient for a family of four.

65. A less disruptive approach, as far as rural lifestyles is concerned, is to increase irrigation efficiency and transfer the conserved water to domestic uses. The "State Water Plan" reports that average irrigation efficiencies in the state range from 21 percent to 35 percent. Clearly a lot of water is being wasted on the farm. It should be noted that much agricultural water is not of potable quality and for domestic use would require treatment or the installation of dual water systems. These systems (where one system delivers potable water and the other delivers water for lawn and garden irrigation) have worked well in a number of northern Utah communities.

66. However, it is important to note that despite a population increase of 62 percent from 1970 to 1990, water consumption in Utah remained virtually constant, due to conservation and increased efficiency. See Utah Foundation, "Research Report" (July 1994), p. 301.

67. It is estimated that one-fourth to one-third of all visitors to Utah's national parks are foreigners. Approximately 20 percent of travel expenditures in the state come from foreign tourists. Source: Utah Office of Planning and Budget, Utah Department of Community and Economic Development, and Bureau of Economic and Business Research at the University of Utah, "EDA Tourism Study" (working draft), 1991.

68. Other states in the Colorado River Basin have expressed the same fear. Such sentiments are rooted in the long and bitter struggle to allocate water from the Colorado River. See Norris Hundley, *Water and the West* (Berkeley: University of California Press, 1975); Philip Fradkin, *A River No More* (Tucson: University of Arizona Press, 1984).

69. Jay M. Bagley, et al., "Impediments to Effective Interactions between Multipurpose Water Districts and Other Governmental Institutions in Urbanizing Areas," Utah Water Research Laboratory, Utah State University, July 1983.

70. Letter from Lynn S. Ludlow, general manager of the Central Utah Water Conservancy District, to Jay M. Bagley, May 25, 1983.

71. Letter from Jay M. Bagley, professor of civil and environmental engineering at Utah State University, to Lynn Ludlow, general manager of the Central Utah Water Conservancy District, May 27, 1983.

72. Upper Colorado River Commission, "Twenty-Fifth Annual Report" Salt Lake City, September 30, 1973, p. 26.

CHAPTER TWO

Water Development in Salt Lake Valley: 1847–1985

Kurt Vedder

This chapter provides a historical overview of Utah water policy from the days of the pioneers to the 1985 CUP repayment election. The specific focus is on the Salt Lake Valley (home of nearly one-half of the state's population) and to a lesser extent Utah County. Both valleys are served by the Provo River and its tributaries[1] (see Fig. 2.1). This chapter also describes the history and physical features of the Central Utah Project; it would be impossible to understand modern Utah water politics without a thorough understanding of how this project came about and how it physically works. A final section discusses the implications of Utah's water history for the future of the state.

Three Eras of Utah Water History

The development of water in Utah can be divided roughly into three periods: mountain and stream development from 1847 to 1879; canals and exchanges, 1879 to 1935; and major transbasin transfers, 1935 to 1985.

Mountain Stream Development, 1847–1879

Brigham Young entered the Salt Lake Valley, then part of Mexico, on July 24, 1847, and proclaimed "this is the place" for the Mormons to settle. Two days before the main party entered the valley, an advance party camped on City Creek where the historic City and County Building now stands. They dug furrows for planting of potatoes, and diverted the stream onto the soil.[2] Utahns have been assiduously developing water supplies ever since and have often thought on a very large scale. At one time early in the territory's history, a design called for a vast system of canals and rivers to link the territory with the rest of the nation, thereby allowing potential settlers to travel much of the overland distance to Utah by barge.[3]

When the Mormon pioneers first entered the valley, their water supply consisted entirely of City Creek, the northernmost creek in the Salt Lake Valley (see Fig. 2.1). It was along this creek, now diverted at the mouth of the canyon into storm drains, that the first settlements were built, and where the downtown area of modern Salt Lake City is located. By the spring of 1848, communities had developed in the southern part of the valley on every major creek and along the Jordan River. For the first thirty years, communities were small and were able to survive on the low creek flows that follow the spring run-offs. But by the 1870s, the initial party of several dozen pioneers had grown to a valley population of about forty thousand, and there was a pressing need to provide more irrigation water during the low flow periods of summer and early autumn.

Canals and Exchanges, 1879–1935

The mountain creeks were fully appropriated for agricultural use by 1860. In response, artesian wells were drilled for the first time in 1864, and remain a significant water source today. In the same year, the idea of a major canal diverting water out of Utah Lake was first introduced. Brigham Young spoke of the "beneficial results that would accrue by irrigating and cultivating an increased amount of land." He said that "the bringing of the waters of Utah Lake would be a means of sustaining a population in Great Salt Lake County of one hundred thousand inhabitants."[4]

In 1879 Salt Lake City began building the Jordan and Salt Lake City Canal across eastern Salt Lake County. The canal-

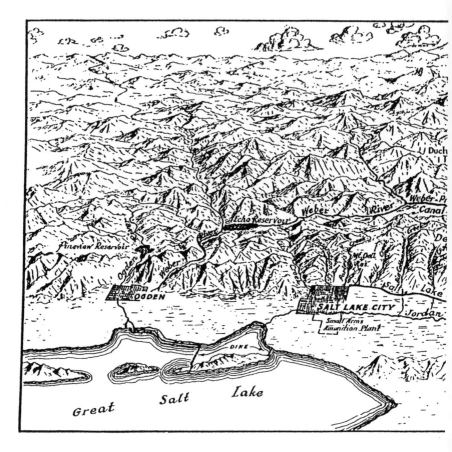

Figure 2.1. The Provo River Project

(from Harris, *100 Years of Water Development [1942]*)

stretched from the Jordan River Narrows at the southernmost point of the valley all the way to the Eagle Gate in downtown Salt Lake City. The 28-mile canal took three years to build. An engineering marvel, it nonetheless failed to supply drinking water to the growing community. Like the Great Salt Lake, Utah Lake is shallow, with a high evaporation rate. It has an outlet, the Jordan River, which traverses the Salt Lake Valley from south to north and empties into the Great Salt Lake, but the water has a high level of solids, making it unpotable without prohibitively expensive treatment. As a result, through the years Utah Lake water has been used only for irrigation.[5]

Concurrent with settling Salt Lake City, the pioneers fanned out into the valley. They dug irrigation ditches and diverted water from Wasatch streams onto their farmlands; water rights were established as early as 1848 on these streams. When Salt Lake City grew to the point that it needed water from a new stream outside the city limits, Parley's Creek was already supplying several farms and orchards. The city offered the irrigators its Utah Lake water in the Jordan and Salt Lake City Canal in exchange for the higher quality canyon water. The irrigators welcomed the exchange agreement because it guaranteed a continuous water supply; when they relied solely on canyon flows, they often ran short of water late in the growing season or during droughts. Thus the exchange agreement helped the farmers obtain a continuous water supply for irrigation and helped the city increase its quantity of culinary water.

The first exchange agreement was reached in 1888 when the city and the Parley's Water Users Association entered into a contract to trade water flowing from Parley's Creek for water flowing in the Jordan and Salt Lake City Canal. A dozen years later a similar exchange was made with the appropriators of Big Cottonwood Creek. This was followed by exchanges on the remaining creeks in the valley, Mill Creek and Little Cottonwood, during the 1920s. Each exchange is unique, but basically they require the city to provide both culinary water from a piped distribution system and irrigation water from Utah Lake to the farmers within the irrigation company boundaries.

Although these exchanges date back several decades, and the exchange waters now flow through a few suburban gardens rather than expansive farms and orchards, they are very much in force today. In 1922, the sixth year of a drought, the waters of Utah Lake dropped so low that the Utah Lake Pumping Station feeding the exchange canals had to quit pumping. However, to continue to fulfill the agreements and preserve its rights to the various mountain streams, Salt Lake City was forced to divert treated culinary water into the canals—even though most of the water is not used, but flows through the ditches and mostly into gutters and storm drains.

Major Transbasin Transfers, 1935–1985

The system of canals and exchange agreements served the Salt Lake Valley well until the 1920s. At that time it became apparent that other sources of water would be needed to meet the needs of the expanding population. Water authorities began to look outside the Salt Lake area for additional sources.

The largest water source south of Salt Lake City is the Provo River. Located outside the Salt Lake Valley, the Provo River drains the southwest corner of the Uinta Mountains, flows into Utah Valley between Provo and Orem, then empties into Utah Lake. Salt Lake City formed the Metropolitan Water District of Salt Lake City (Metro) in 1935 to contract with the United States Bureau of Reclamation to build the Provo River Project, which consists of Deer Creek Reservoir and related facilities. Metro provides wholesale water service to half a million residents in Salt Lake City, the unincorporated east bench, and Sandy City. These three combined areas effectively cover the east side of the Salt Lake Valley.

The Deer Creek Project was proposed by a task force in 1929 and endorsed by city voters in a 1937 bond election. Although city residents embarked almost alone on this project in the midst of the Great Depression (other major players such as Salt Lake County and the state of Utah refused to participate), a drought in the early 1930s (1934 was the driest year in northern Utah history) made the project essential in the voters' eyes. The resulting 150,000 acre-foot Deer Creek Reservoir is filled almost entirely with water transferred into the basin from the Weber River and the Duchesne River. Because of earlier appropriations by Provo

City and other Utah Valley cities, only a small portion of Provo River water is used, even though the reservoir straddles the Provo. Most of the project's water is then transferred out of the Provo River Basin through an aqueduct to the Salt Lake Valley. These diversions represent Utah's first significant effort to move water from one major river basin to another.

Even before the Deer Creek Reservoir system was completed, plans were made to expand the diversion idea and enlarge the Provo River Project to include Utah's share of the water in the Colorado River Basin. The Green River, the largest tributary of the Colorado, drains the eastern portion of Utah, then joins the Colorado River near Moab. In northeastern Utah, the Duchesne River drains the Uintah Basin before flowing into the Green River (see Fig. 2.2).

The basic strategy for what would eventually become the Central Utah Project was set decades ago: get Utah's share of Colorado River water over the Wasatch Mountains and into the Wasatch Front. Documents from the era show the strategy was in place to divert Colorado River water immediately after the signing of the 1948 Upper Colorado River Compact, although the reservoirs initially envisioned were along the Colorado River itself as far east as Wyoming and Colorado.[6] The Central Utah Project would eventually tap the Colorado River tributaries along the Uinta mountains, many miles west of the Colorado and much closer to major Utah cities.

The CUP has been the central element of water plans since the 1960s. Wasatch Mountain streams and the Deer Creek project deliver water to the east side of the Salt Lake Valley. But the west side of the valley, which has no significant streams and was not urbanized until recently, has significantly less water. As a result, wells have been dug and other mountain stream–irrigation water exchanges have been worked out.

Eliminating the consideration of alternatives to the CUP from the onset, Utah's water strategy has been consistent since World War II: "The water problems of Salt Lake City and adjacent municipalities are only temporarily solved because of the Deer Creek project. Unusual growth in Salt Lake City and the state must wait on the Central Utah Project."[7]

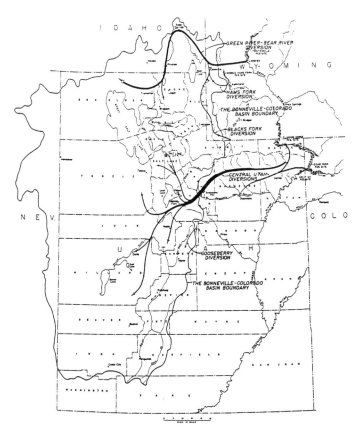

Figure 2.2. Potential Transmountain Water Diversions: Colorado River
Basin to Bonneville Basin. (*Water for Utah,* 1948)

The Central Utah Project

The Central Utah Project is the centerpiece of Utah's
water development policy in the latter half of the twentieth century; it has dominated the policy agenda of Utah's congressional
delegation during this period. The project was authorized over
three decades ago as one of several projects in the Colorado
River Storage Project Act of 1956, passed to utilize the Colorado
River water rights of the "upper basin" states of Colorado, Utah,

New Mexico, and Wyoming, as well as the more populous "lower basin" states of California, Nevada, and Arizona. In 1922 these two artificial basins were designated by the Colorado River Compact.[8] Each basin was allotted 7.5 million acre-feet of water, with the powerful lower basin states allotted an extra 1 million acre-feet even though these states contribute next to nothing to the Colorado River's flow. In 1948 the state of Utah was allotted 1.7 million acre-feet in the equally contentious Upper Colorado River Basin Compact. The CUP is designed to utilize part of Utah's share of the Colorado River.[9]

Although no specific plans were in place for the CUP when the 1956 act became law, partial funding for each of the six units of the CUP was appropriated over the next ten years. The plan for the Bonneville Unit, by far the largest and most complex unit, was first formalized in 1964.[10] Funding for this unit has accounted for over 90 percent of CUP appropriations over the years. In 1965, the voters in the seven original counties in the Central Utah Water Conservancy District, including Salt Lake and Utah counties, voted for the project by a 93 percent to 7 percent margin, allowing the District to use property taxes, in addition to water sale revenues, to partially repay the federal government.[11]

After this early high point, the history of the CUP has been one of perpetual crisis; from 1956 to the present, there has been an unbroken series of impediments to construction of the project.

The first crisis was a fiscal one; congressional appropriations did not begin in earnest until the late 1960s and early 1970s (Fig. 2.3) and then grew steadily up to 1989. Just as funding had begun to stabilize in the 1970s, the National Environmental Protection Act (NEPA) was passed. NEPA required "environmental impact statements" of all major federal projects. This provided the opportunity for environmental groups, which had not mobilized during the 1965 vote, to question the project. Nonetheless, the Bonneville Unit and the rest of the CUP moved through the environmental impact process essentially unchanged, although Utah Lake diking was dropped.[12] It was not until the early 1990s that environmentalists were able to force major changes in the project, with new requirements for

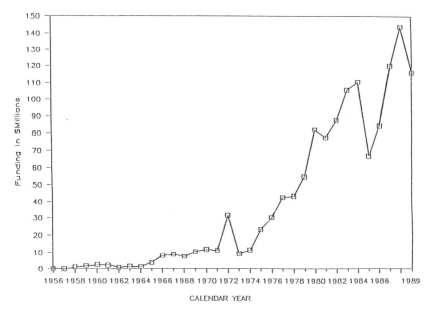

Figure 2.3 Central Utah Project Funding (in nominal dollars).

wildlife habitat preservation, instream flow minimums, and conditional provisions for further irrigation development.

A second long-standing crisis developed around the numerous attempts to work out a settlement between the Northern Ute Tribe and the CUP sponsors. As explained in chapter one, the Indian units of the CUP were necessary to compensate for water being diverted to the non-Indian Bonneville Unit. The 1965 deferral agreement allowed this water to be used for the Wasatch Front in return for Indian water projects in the Colorado River Basin where they live. In the 1970s and again in the late 1980s, the Indians threatened to stop the project and reclaim their water rights. Efforts are now under way to finalize a negotiated settlement and a compact between the tribe, the District, the state, and the federal government.

The most public threat to the CUP came in 1977, when the newly elected President Jimmy Carter issued his "hit list" of western water projects to be cut or curtailed; elements of the Bonneville Unit were contained in this list. However, the strength of western water interests proved to be much too powerful, and the CUP enjoyed increasing appropriations every year of the Carter presidency.

Another crisis the CUP faced was the repayment battle fought through the 1970s up to the 1985 election, which approved a new repayment contract for the project. A contract adding about $370 million to the $2 billion project became necessary when inflationary pressures and cost overruns pushed costs well over the original authorization ceiling. The District and various government agencies attempted to reduce the cost of CUP by selling off portions of the project to other government bodies and creating a large power project to provide supplementary revenues. These efforts were designed to reduce the amount of money the public would have to approve in the new contract.[13]

It was largely the pressures resulting from this series of crises that forced CUP sponsors to modify the project and greatly reduce its size and scope (see Fig. 2.4). These open conflicts over the project also began to erode public confidence in the CUP. Approval for the project dropped from 93 percent to 72 percent when the election was finally held in 1985. Although many groups were now against the project, ranging from environmental organizations to antitax crusaders, the opposition never coalesced, and the new repayment contract was approved.[14] The latest crisis played itself out in the 102d Congress. Although voters approved the more costly revised version of CUP in 1985, until late in 1992 Congress had not. In that year Congress reauthorized the project at the new ceiling so that yearly appropriations could continue. (Chapter nine reviews this struggle for reauthorization.)

A full understanding of the Central Utah Project requires an explanation of its physical as well as political features. Laying out the project demonstrates how municipal, irrigation, and Indian water interests are arranged and also allows the opportunity to clarify several misconceptions about the project (see Fig. 2.4). The project is divided into two major components: the Bonneville Unit, which transfers water from the Uinta Basin to the Great Basin, and the project units that serve local areas of the Uinta Basin.

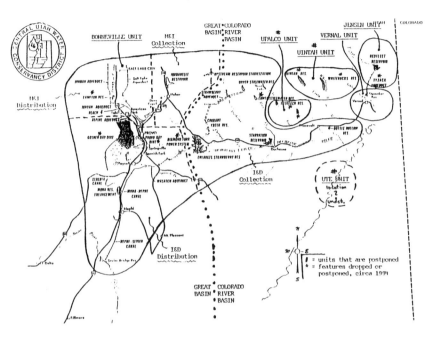

Figure 2.4. Central Utah Project (CUP brochure, ca. 1980).

Bonneville Unit

The Bonneville Unit is the largest, costliest, and most controversial unit in the CUP. It contains several large mountain reservoirs, used for water storage and recreation, and over a hundred miles of aqueducts, tunnels, and canals to deliver the water to various users. When President Carter put his water project "hit list" together in 1976, this was the only CUP unit included.

Although the fact is not generally known, the Great Basin portion of the Bonneville Unit consists of two distinct halves, each with two subunits (see Fig. 2.4). The M&I half consists of the Jordanelle Reservoir, which collects municipal and industrial water for the cities of the Wasatch Front, and the Jordan Aqueduct, which delivers this M&I water to the Salt Lake

Valley. The irrigation half consists of the Strawberry Reservoir and its collection system in the Colorado River Basin, which gathers irrigation and drainage (I&D) water for farming in eastern, central, and southern Utah, and a distribution system designed to deliver this I&D water to Great Basin farmers.

A clear distinction between water for M&I (cities) and I&D (farmers) can be made because the sources of the water are different. The 132,000 acre-feet of I&D water comes from an interbasin diversion; it diverts water from the Colorado River Basin into the Great Basin. In other words, the CUP's irrigation water is from Colorado River Basin streams, which would otherwise flow downstream (through the Uintah and Ouray Indian Reservation) to the Lower Basin. In contrast, the 95,000 acre-feet of M&I water comes primarily from increased water storage of Great Basin water; it captures spring runoff and releases it when needed. The only link between the M&I and I&D projects is the water the latter puts into Utah Lake to replace water removed from the Provo River by the former. Otherwise, the two elements are essentially severable and independent.[15]

Then why are these two separate water projects in the same unit of CUP? The M&I and I&D systems are combined for political and economic reasons. The populous area in the north that will be served by the M&I system helps provide political clout, and the rural central Utah irrigation was included to provide nearly $1 billion in federal power revenues for project construction.

A major source of CUP funding is the Upper Colorado River Basin Fund. The federal government collects hydropower revenues from Colorado River Storage Project (CRSP) dams (such as Hoover and Glen Canyon) for irrigation projects in area states. Without these funds it would be impossible for Utah farmers to afford water development. Farming accounts for only 2 percent of Utah's gross state product and continues to decline in importance in the urbanizing Utah economy.[16] Using CRSP funds, the farmers were eligible to obtain $956,138,000 in financing for the irrigation component of the Bonneville Unit, but were required to pay back only $16,400,000. Moreover, the irrigators repay this amount over fifty years at no interest.[17] They will pay this small sum because under federal law, farmers are required to pay only what they can afford, and crops such as alfalfa have low value. In terms of the Utah contribution, users of the M&I water repay about one-half of the costs, while the I&D water was intended to be more or less "free"; the federal government pays the rest.

Currently, three of the four elements of the Bonneville Unit are nearing completion. The first element, the M&I collection system, is in place. Construction of the $353 million Jordanelle Dam and reservoir proceeded despite lingering concerns that the dam is located on an earthquake fault. The dam was topped off in late 1992 and is being filled. The completion of this dam was necessary before large water deliveries from the 94,750 acre-foot M&I part of the unit could be made to Wasatch Front cities. The second element, the Jordan Aqueduct, which delivers water to west Salt Lake Valley, constitutes the M&I distribution system and was completed in the mid-1980s. It was then promptly sold to the two Salt Lake Valley water wholesalers, Metro and the Salt Lake County Water Conservancy District, to lower the total debt of CUP and delay the repayment crisis.

The third element, the I&D collection portion that will gather Colorado River streams through a series of aqueducts and mountain reservoirs, is almost finished. The Utah water managers' decades-old dream of a "spigot" to divert Colorado River water into the Great Basin and out of the hands of lower basin states, particularly powerful California, is almost in place. Some of the water coming from the Uinta Basin will also be used to replace Provo River water diverted into the M&I system—another reason why the I&D collection system has been built quickly.

This brings us to the fourth element of the Bonneville Unit. In contrast to the I&D collection system (which delivers most of its water to Strawberry Reservoir), the I&D aqueducts designed to deliver water from Strawberry Reservoir to farms in central and southern Utah have not been started.[18] This distribution portion of the I&D unit is not popular in Congress, and the provisions in the CUP Completion Act for building the I&D are less generous than those of past plans. If it is not built, and perhaps even if it is, tens of thousands of acre-feet of heavily subsidized I&D water may ultimately be transferred to M&I use instead, thereby freeing up water that could serve urban residents. This transfer of water rights to "higher" (meaning more economical) use is a quickly developing trend in Arizona, Colorado, California, and other western states, occurring when water can be sold at a higher price elsewhere, which is often the case with affluent urbanized areas. However, state law requires the seller to demonstrate that the transfer does no harm to third party water users, and some rural users have a deep-seated aversion to selling their water rights.

Unique environmental and economic conditions have forced the alteration of the two remaining major components of the original Bonneville Unit.[19] First, the proposed diking of the naturally formed Utah Lake in the Great Basin will probably never occur. Environmentalists have long opposed diking, and flooding in the early 1980s helped kill the proposal; with the extremely high levels of rainfall, attention centered not on how to save water in the lake, but how to get rid of it. The diking would have reduced the size of Utah Lake by about one-half, significantly reducing the evaporative loss of water, but also destroying thousands of acres of prime wetlands and wildlife habitat.

Although the water from Utah Lake is difficult to purify for culinary purposes, the mountain streams that feed it are easily treated. Through an exchange, the irrigator-owned stream water was to be diverted for culinary use, with the lake water, which was to be "saved" from evaporation through diking, used for irrigation. The Bureau of Reclamation planned to facilitate this exchange by purchasing stock in irrigation companies to obtain their water. Opponents of the CUP have long suggested transfers as an alternative water source, observing that no complex and costly structures are necessary for the culinary use of water exchanged for Utah Lake water, and there is a decreasing demand for irrigation along the urbanizing Wasatch Front.

Another CUP component, the Diamond Fork power system, was to be part of the irrigation system of the Bonneville Unit. It was designed to generate electrical power from diverted streamflows as they fall from the mountainous Colorado River Basin to the lower Great Basin, where the water is eventually delivered by pipeline for I&D purposes. At one time, project planners had hoped to sell electricity from a 1,200-megawatt power system (which is about one-third the total current generating capacity in the entire state of Utah) to help pay for the Central Utah Project and delay renegotiating a repayment contract with the federal government. But the existing power supply is ample, and no one would purchase power from the project, forcing the commercial hydropower plan to be abandoned.

The CUP Completion Act authorized $150 million to complete a reduced version of the I&D distribution portion of the unit, consisting of a single pipeline from Spanish Fork Canyon to the Sevier River Basin. The Act stipulates that binding contracts must be signed for at least 90 percent of the irrigation water before construction begins. Other I&D features, such as the now canceled $53 million CUP Mosida pumping project for Utah Valley, will have to come from state or private sources.

Colorado River Basin Units

Located in the upper Colorado River Basin, the Uinta Basin units consist of several small projects, typically a dam or two, each of which provides water for a localized area.

While often thought of as projects designed to compensate interests which lost water to the Bonneville Unit, the Uinta Basin units of the CUP are in fact self-contained, built to serve the small communities east of Salt Lake City—with one large exception. The Ute Indians were promised various projects that would replace by 2005 the approximately 50,000 acre-feet of Indan water that is being diverted to the Bonneville Unit. The Upalco, Uintah, Ute, and even the Bonneville Unit originally contained provisions to compensate the Indians for their lost water. However, the first three units have been indefinitely deferred and are not likely to be built, and the dam designed primarily for Indian use in the Bonneville Unit, the Lower Stillwater, has been dropped.

Moving from west to east, the five other units of the Central Utah Project are the Upalco, Uintah, Ute Indian, Vernal, and Jensen. In 1965 the Upalco Unit was to consist of two reservoirs, then a single one, and is now on indefinite hold. Funding for this unit has stopped. The original delay came when Indian lands were needed to build the single reservoir. Indian leaders continued to balk at providing the land until questions surrounding the Ute Indian Unit of the CUP were resolved (see discussion below). The CUP Completion Act provides no new authorization for this project, essentially killing it.

Authorization for the Uintah Unit did not come until 1968 (all other units of the CUP except the Ute Indian Unit were authorized in 1956). Like the Upalco Unit, it was scaled back from a dual to a single reservoir project and is now on indefinite hold. Appropriations for the Uintah Unit through the years have averaged only a few hundred thousand dollars per year to continue planning studies and pay for staff. The Uintah Unit was to provide most of its water for Indian needs, as well as to Roosevelt City and several smaller non-Indian communities.

An early version of the CUP Completion Act attempted to revive this unit. The bill stated that the Uintah Unit's $192,760,000 of unspent authorization from the 1956 act was still available for use and authorized expenditures for two large reservoirs and several smaller dams and projects. In essence, interests in the Uinta Basin asked for everything, hoping to get something, and the Utah congressional delegation complied by putting their "wish list" in the bill.

It soon became clear, however, that the large dams proposed for the original Uintah and Upalco Units were a political liability. Bowing to political necessity, both the Upalco and Uintah Units were replaced by the Uinta Basin Replacement project, which was authorized by the 1992 Completion Act. It is now generally accepted that the large dams envisioned in the original plans for these two units will never be built.[20] Instead, the replacement project offers a number of small-scale reservoirs and channel rehabilitations. In February 1995, the District identified specific proposed projects for the Uinta Basin; they must now complete an environmental impact statement.

The Ute Indian Unit was originally proposed to develop remaining Utah water in the Colorado River for use by the Northern Ute Tribe. This unit never emerged from the planning phase; it progressed so slowly the Bureau never even developed a proposal identifying what reservoirs or aqueducts might be built, or where they might be located. Through the years the Bureau of Reclamation showed little interest in building this project, and construction was never authorized by Congress. The CUP Completion Act provides a settlement for the tribe in lieu of this project.

The Vernal Unit was completed in 1962. As it was finished before regular appropriations for any of the other projects had begun, it no doubt would have been completed without being an element of the CUP. Its primary component is a single reservoir that provides irrigation and municipal water to the small communities of Vernal, Naples, and Maeser.

The Jensen Unit, like the Vernal Unit, is essentially complete. It is a single reservoir unit designed primarily to provide municipal and industrial water to the small town of Jensen, near the Utah-Colorado border.

The Much-Revised CUP

The Central Utah Project's history has been a difficult one since its inception. Fiscal problems have plagued the project since the beginning, forcing major changes in the project, and they now threaten the irrigation component—two-thirds of the Bonneville Unit in terms of acre-feet of water—in spite of the assiduous cultivation of relevant water constituencies.

The success of the project in generating appropriations has varied greatly, depending on whether a feature has been planned to benefit an Indian reservation, rural, or urban users. The Northern Utes have experienced the greatest difficulty in attracting funding, in part because of their small population (approximately twenty-five hundred). If the Ute settlement is implemented, it will be the first time the tribe has actually received substantial benefits from the CUP.

Rural water development has been more successful, largely because rural communities served by the CUP involve around fifty thousand people and the collection system can be converted to urban use. The economic contribution of farming areas is modest, but they have a long-standing political presence in Washington and the state legislature. In the current political climate, however, western agricultural interests have experienced increasing difficulty in generating more funding for western irrigation.

The Bonneville I&D collection system has been supported by both urban and rural political interests because it takes "Utah" water out of the Colorado River Basin, and therefore out of California's hands, and places it in Utah's Great Basin. It was the compulsion to build this transbasin diversion that was the motivation for the CUP in the 1950s. The Bonneville I&D collection system is nearly completed, with only the Diamond Fork diversion system remaining. This diversion would take Strawberry Reservoir water south through pipelines to the Spanish Fork River. With this diversion, the "spigot" will be in place to take water from the Colorado River into the Great Basin. If the I&D interests are bought out, it is still possible that a proposed tunnel (the Wallsburg Tunnel) could be built to transfer Strawberry Reservoir water to Wasatch Front cities. This would allow the irrigation collection system to be converted into part of the urban water network.[21]

Forces driving municipal water development have been the strongest. There are nearly one million people served by the M&I portion of CUP. The Salt Lake area also contains the state capital and much of the state's business, cultural, media, and religious activities. Water for city use could expand if irrigation water in the CUP is purchased and diverted to the Wasatch Front.

Future Plans for Water Development in Utah

Even before CUP deliveries are made, the state is already developing plans to import Bear River water from 100 miles north of Salt Lake City into the metropolitan area—this time using state funds exclusively.

The Bear River begins in the northwest part of the Uinta Mountains in Utah, flows north through Wyoming and Idaho, and then turns back south into Utah, emptying into the northern end of the Great Salt Lake. Like the Colorado, the Bear is an interstate river, which may compel Utah water decision makers to develop "our" water before it is taken by an out-of-state entity.

Planning documents of the state of Utah indicate that Salt Lake County, with nearly one-half of the state's population, has sufficient water resources with CUP to last until 2020 under current high water-use patterns. At that time, the Bear River Basin Plan proposes to divert 100,000 acre-feet of water a year south to the Wasatch Front. The plan projects a total price tag of about a quarter billion dollars and a cost-to-benefit ratio barely over 1:1.[22]

Somewhat encouraging to critics of large water development projects is the exclusive state and local funding. Without the advantage of extremely low-interest federal dollars to subsidize the Bear River Plan, alternatives, including conservation, are more likely to be pursued.

Indeed, another recent report released by the state does identify competing alternatives. Although conservation induced by higher water rates is dismissed, the study indicates that unused irrigation water in Utah Lake could be used in dual water systems at about the same price as Bear River water (irrigation water for outside residential use, culinary water for inside use).[23] If there is a push to develop Utah's share of the Bear River water, the state may repeat much of its experience with the Central Utah Project through a similarly controversial, expansive, and expensive "Northern Utah Project" that would seek to meet water needs with a supply-side solution. The dramatic revisions to the CUP brought about by the federal government's new 35 percent local cost-sharing provisions would strongly suggest that the "100 percent local cost share" of Bear River development would similarly result in major revisions to this project.

With the state's continuing economic and population growth, the politics of water in Utah will always be exciting. Water policy changes quite dramatically in response to rapidly changing political developments at both the national and state level. For example, the implementation of the CUP Completion Act has been an exercise in quick response; as one water planner put it, "with CUP water we are now shooting at a moving target."

Notes

1. For an overview of the major water system serving the northern part of the Wasatch Front, see Richard W. Sadler and Richard C. Roberts, *The Weber Basin: Grass Roots Democracy and Water Development* (Logan: Utah State University Press, 1994).

2. Fisher Sanford Harris, *100 Years of Water Development* (Salt Lake City: Metropolitan Water District, 1942).

3. John Sweeny Harvey, "A Historical Overview of the Evolutions of Institutions Dealing With Water Resource Use, and Water Resource Development in Utah—1847 through 1947" (master's thesis, Utah State University, 1989).

4. Harris, *100 Years of Water Development*, p. 3.

5. "Blending" low-quality Jordan River water with high-quality water supplies was tried as recently as the summer of 1992. However, the experiment immediately failed, as bacteria began growing in the blended water. The main aqueduct serving the west Salt Lake Valley had to be closed until it was completely flushed.

6. Utah Water and Power Board, "Water for Utah for Full Development of Utah's Resources" (1948).

7. Rene N. Ballard, "The Salt Lake Metropolitan Water District" (Salt Lake City: University of Utah Institute of Government, December 1948), p. 14.

8. For background see Norris Hundley, *Water and the West: The Colorado River Compact and the Politics of Water in the American Way* (Berkeley: University of California Press, 1975).

9. Marc Reisner, *Cadillac Desert: The American West and Its Disappearing Water* (New York: Viking, 1987), pp. 129–30.

10. U.S. Bureau of Reclamation, *Central Utah Project, Bonneville Unit Definite Plan Report* (Salt Lake City: 1964); and *Bonneville Unit: Revised Supplement to the Definite Plan Report* (Salt Lake City: 1984).

11. It should be noted that the financing provisions for the municipal and industrial portion of the project are quite favorable, with a repayment period of forty years and 3.22 percent interest. The repayment provisions of the irrigation and drainage (I&D) portion of the project are even more favorable, with farmers repaying $16 million of about $1 billion in I&D costs, at no interest over fifty years.

12. U.S. Bureau of Reclamation, *Central Utah Project Bonneville Unit, Final Environmental Statement* (Salt Lake City: 1973).

13. Jon R. Miller, "The Political Economy of Western Water Finance: Cost Allocation and the Bonneville Unit of the Central Utah Project," *American Journal of Agricultural Economics* (May 1987): 303–10.

14. John G. Francis and Brian Hatch, "The CUP Half Full: An Analysis of Voter and Interest Group Support at the Intrastate Level" (paper presented at the 1986 Western Social Science Association Meeting, Reno, Nev.).

15. The 1992 CUP Completion Act authorizes a study of the proposed Wallsburg Tunnel, which would link the M&I and I&D portions of the project and permit a reallocation of water from the latter to the former.

16. Utah State Economic Coordinating Committee, *Economic Report to the Governor* (Salt Lake City: 1989), p. 54.

17. The other sources of funds for the $1,948,841,000 Bonneville Unit are:

$16,949,000 from power sales; $481,895,000 from the M&I part of the unit, mostly from property taxes and water sales; and $477,459,000, which is "fact sheet non-reimbursable" by project users and paid by the federal government (report compiled by U.S. Bureau of Reclamation, Upper Colorado Region [Salt Lake City, 1989], p. 353).

18. The District has initiated preliminary engineering studies for the I&D delivery system. The definite plan report is due in August 1996. The District hopes to begin construction of the pipeline to Juab County in early 1997. See *CUP Newsletter* (Spring 1994): 2.

19. Miller, "The Political Economy of Western Water Finance."

20. A recent publication from the District explains that the purpose of the Uinta Basin Replacement project "is to increase efficiency, enhance beneficial uses, and achieve greater water conservation within the Uinta Basin by developing project features which are more feasible and environmentally less damaging than the large reservoirs planned by the Bureau of Reclamation." Central Utah Water Conservancy District, "Central Utah Project Completion Act, Uinta Basin Replacement Projects," memo announcing public scoping meetings (Orem, Utah, January 1993).

21. The I&D component has been scaled back and renamed the Spanish Fork–Nephi Supplemental Irrigation System. A feasibility study for the Wallsburg Tunnel was initiated in early 1995.

22. Utah Division of Water Resources, *Utah State Water Plan: Bear River Basin* (1992).

23. Utah Division of Water Resources, *Evaluations of Water Needs and Supply Options for Salt Lake, Davis and Weber Counties* (Salt Lake City: 1992).

PART II

Conflict over Priorities:
The Central Utah Project

Without the Central Utah Water Conservancy District, there would be no CUP. When the Reclamation Act was passed in 1902, it was obvious that the federal government could not administer all the projects it planned to build. To solve this problem, the act required project beneficiaries to form a water district or association, so that the Reclamation Service (later the Bureau of Reclamation) could turn over the projects to them when they completed construction. But another duty, perhaps even more important, fell to these water organizations; they became an important source of political support for the fledgling federal reclamation program. Over time, these water districts sprang up all over the West, and they became increasingly adept at lobbying Congress and the executive branch.

There are nearly a thousand special water districts in the United States, 95 percent of which are in the seventeen western states.[1] David Getches provides a succinct description of these districts:

> Irrigation districts [also known as conservancy, conservation, reclamation, or water control districts] are formed under special provisions of state law and enjoy a governmental or quasi-governmental status; yet most have a certain degree of autonomy exempting them from much public accountability. Irrigation districts distribute about half of all water used in the West, giving them economic power. Many also have lobbying organizations and political influence.[2]

Of the dozens of special water districts in Utah, the three largest along the Wasatch Front are the Central Utah Water Conservancy District, the Salt Lake County Water Conservancy District, and the Metropolitan Water District of Salt Lake City. According to economist Jon Miller, these three districts collected $333,506,624 in taxes from 1965 to 1991. Of that amount, the Central Utah Water Conservancy District collected the lion's share, $229,904,168.[3] Special water districts usually do not attract a great deal of attention, but they certainly attract a lot of tax revenue.

As Carrie Ulrich and Terry Holzworth point out in chapter three, you cannot understand western water politics without understanding water districts. Ulrich and Holzworth write about the Central Utah Water Conservancy District, which has had a sometimes convulsive history. At one time it was virtually free of outside interference; even though it was funded by the taxpayers, there was little opportunity for public input. As a result, the District occasionally made decisions that served its needs quite well but were arguably not in the public interest. As water policy changed in the 1970s and 1980s, the District came under increasing criticism. Critics argued that it was unresponsive to outside input, especially if the input came from groups that were not part of the District's traditional constituency. Slowly it began to change, however, and over a period of two decades has undergone some significant reforms.

The political transformation of the District is not simply an interesting theoretical issue; the District currently collects nearly $14 million in property taxes and $1.2 million in water charges each year.[4] And politically the District is more important than ever; the 1992 CUP Completion Act authorized the District to be the official builder of the project and an official entity of the federal government. In the past the District took orders from the Bureau of Reclamation; now it is the other way around. This change presents an opportunity to address an interesting political question: How do we get an "unresponsive" government entity to respond? Carrie Ulrich and Terry Holzworth help answer this question by examining the political events that ultimately forced the District to change.

The story of the CUWCD is followed by Roy Ramthun's chapter on Jordanelle State Park. He proves the old adage that where there is water, there is conflict over water. This is certainly the case in regard to the park which is currently under construction at Jordanelle Reservoir. Roy explains how two sets of beneficiaries—the public and developers—fought to control development at the park site, with the Division of State Parks finding itself squarely in the middle.

There is a common theme in these two chapters: the relationship between public input and government policy. Do interest groups help us gain access to government, or do they simply usurp control over policy-making? Who has the greatest influence over the governmental entities that make critically important decisions regarding water?

Notes

1. Charles Meyers, A. Dan Tarlock, James Corbridge, Jr., and David Getches, *Water Resource Management*, 3d ed. (Mineola, NY: The Foundation Press, 1988), p. 731.

2. David Getches, *Water Law in a Nutshell*, 2d ed. (St. Paul, Minn.: West Publishing Co., 1990), pp. 429–30.

3. Jon R. Miller, "On the Economics of Western Local Water Finance: The Central Utah Experience," *Land Economics* 69 (August 1993): 299–303.

4. The District's total 1993 revenue collection, including property taxes and water sales, totaled $33,010,944. Central Utah Water Conservancy District, "Annual Report" (Orem, Utah, 1993), p. 17. For fiscal year 1996 the District requested $40 million in federal revenues.

CHAPTER THREE

Opening the Water Bureaucracy

Carrie L. Ulrich and

R. Terry Holzworth

⁷ The Central Utah Water Conservancy District was created in 1964 to finance and manage the Central Utah Project. The District received overwhelming public support in the 1965 referendum to approve the project's initial federal repayment contract. From that point on, however, the District has managed the construction of the CUP with little public interest or involvement. By the early 1980s, as the project extended beyond its original completion date, critics began to question the District's responsiveness. In particular, they charged that the District was unresponsive to local government, the general public, and certain financial and environmental aspects of the CUP.

Critics have forced fundamental changes in the District, changes which have made it more responsive and more responsible as it completes the CUP. This chapter discusses five areas in which the District has changed: the appointment process for the District's board of directors; the District's daily operations, including capital management and board oversight; the District's attitude toward interests such as environmentalists and Native Americans, who have traditionally opposed the CUP; the District's level of responsibility for constructing the project; and the District's interest in soliciting public input. The chapter concludes with an analysis of the forces that can change a non-elected, seemingly unresponsive government agency.

Original Mission and Repayment Strategies

The District's original mission was simply water development. It was created under Utah's Water Conservancy Act to develop the state's share of the Colorado River through the Central Utah Project. The District represented Utah water users to the Bureau of Reclamation, which was responsible for building the CUP and receiving federal appropriations allocated to the project. In short, the District was supposed to be an advocate for Utah residents, advising the Bureau on what CUP features should be built to satisfy Utah's water needs.

While the District did not actually build the CUP, it did have the power to market CUP water and raise revenue to repay the Bureau for the project. The District was authorized to sell CUP water to irrigation companies, municipalities, and other water conservancy districts; to collect water use fees and ad valorem taxes from water users and taxpayers in the District; and to repay the cost of the CUP to the federal government.

The board originally had seventeen members: eight from the urban Salt Lake and Utah counties and nine from the rural counties of Uintah, Duchesne, Summit, Wasatch, and Juab. This composition was intended to provide a check-and-balance system between rural and urban interests, since the rural counties would have a majority on the board, while the populous urban counties would have veto power through a public referendum.[1] Between 1967 and 1970, the District added two more "rural" board members, but District decisions are rarely decided on a rural versus urban basis. The values and priorities of both rural and urban board members tend to reflect the District's original purpose: to develop Utah's water and build the CUP.[2]

The Central Utah Project's original 1964 repayment contract allocated $102.4 million for the components of the CUP that would provide municipal and industrial water. By 1980 these funds were running out due to rapid inflation, delays in funding, and the Bureau's practice of shifting planning and design funds between projects within the Colorado River Storage Project. No M&I water had been delivered, though it was supposed to have been available by the early 1970s. The key facility for delivering M&I water to Salt Lake and Utah counties, the

Jordanelle Reservoir, had yet to be constructed. The Bureau couldn't request additional funding for the project, because it hadn't determined the actual costs of Jordanelle, and yet the District and the Bureau were apprehensive about stopping construction, because doing so might endanger the federal funding for the project. The agencies needed a way to stretch their current funds until the costs of Jordanelle Reservoir could be determined.

Bureau of Reclamation policy requires that, before it can build an M&I project facility, the intended water users must sign a contract with the Bureau agreeing to repay the cost of the facility. Accordingly, the Central Utah Project's original 1965 Bonneville Unit repayment contract required M&I water users to repay the $102.4 million cost of the CUP's M&I component through taxes and revenue collected by the District.[3]

By the late 1970s, the cost of the M&I component had risen markedly. The Bureau recognized that the 1965 contract would not cover these costs, and in 1980 the Bureau and the District negotiated a supplemental Bonneville Unit repayment contract that would have increased the District's repayment costs.

This contract was never implemented. According to the United States General Accounting Office, the assistant secretary of the interior for land and water rejected the contract because it was "legally questionable, contained several provisions which were not fiscally prudent, and did not adequately disclose the cost of the project to those responsible for repayment."[4] The Bureau and the District were forced to withdraw the contract.

But according to the District's attorney, Edward W. Clyde, the withdrawal was the agencies' idea. He explained that the Bureau had not completed its investigation of the Jordanelle site and did not know what facilities would be constructed there.

> [T]he District and the Bureau thought that it was unfair to the voters to ask them to make an additional debt commitment without our being able to tell them what we were going to construct [at Jordanelle], and what the additional construction cost would be and without providing for them a reasonable estimate of the cost of water. A contract negotiated in 1980 was thus never executed.[5]

Without the supplemental repayment contract, the District and the Bureau had no additional funds for the M&I component, and the existing funds were running out. To continue construction of the project, the agencies passed a resolution invoking the Water Supply Act of 1958. This act allows the Bureau to enlarge a proposed project to store additional M&I water for an anticipated future demand and to defer the cost of the enlargement for up to ten years. In their resolution the agencies designated 60,000 of the 99,000 acre-feet of Jordanelle's M&I water as "future supply." The District's repayment obligation under the 1965 contract was then sufficient to cover the costs of the remaining 39,000 acre-feet of "present supply." Use of the Water Supply Act thus allowed the agencies to continue construction of the Bonneville Unit with nearly two-thirds of the M&I component exempt from a repayment contract.

The District then paid $10 million from its cash reserves to continue construction of the Jordan and Alpine aqueducts, although under the CUP construction agreement, the District was not required to pay construction costs in advance.[6] This payment showed the District's intent to pay for the remaining 60,000 acre-feet of M&I water and also reduced the amount of project costs that the District would have to repay later. The District had these funds available because its policies allowed it to accumulate large cash reserves without designating what they would be used for.

The District's creative use of the Water Supply Act and its $10 million cash advance kept the project moving without additional federal funding. In July 1984, it resumed negotiations with the Bureau, eventually agreeing to increase it's M&I repayment obligation to $554.2 million.[7] This repayment contract would later need to be approved by residents in a referendum.

Two years later, the U.S. General Accounting Office analyzed the Bureau's 1981 resolution and concluded that it had used the Water Supply Act to defer CUP costs above the legal repayment ceiling. After reviewing the legislative history of the act, the GAO determined that the purpose of the act was to encourage construction for uncertain future needs, since it is usually less expensive to build a larger facility than to enlarge a completed facility. However, according to the GAO, the Bureau had used the act to "defer repayment obligations and thereby continue planned construction of facilities for M&I water supply already under contract," which was an entirely different purpose than Congress had intended.[8]

In fact, at the time the District and the Bureau designated 39,000 acre-feet of M&I water as the total "present supply," the District had a contract with the Salt Lake County Water Conservancy District for 50,000 acre-feet of M&I water. Edward W. Clyde explained how the District could apply the label "future supply" to water that was already spoken for: "Generally speaking, when a large multi-purpose project is constructed, there is not an immediate need nor use for all of the municipal water."[9] Clyde also justified using the Water Supply Act, although the proposed project had not been enlarged to store additional M&I water to meet a future demand.[10] At the time the 1965 contract was negotiated, he said, the contracting parties "understood that they were building a project which would develop a municipal water supply for future use, and they anticipated and agreed *at that time* to include storage in the Project to meet that recognized future demand. This is precisely what the G.A.O. report states would be proper."[11]

In contrast, Eugene Riordan, an attorney for the National Wildlife Federation, argued that use of the Water Supply Act is proper only if a project undergoes an operation or design change that makes additional M&I water available. The NWF was concerned about the CUP's environmental impacts and planned to challenge continued funding for the project. According to Riordan, "The Water Supply Act was simply not intended to be used to retrofit the repayment obligation for a project that hasn't changed."[12]

The GAO estimated that if the Bureau had deferred the cost of the 60,000 acre-feet for the full ten years, the federal government could have lost up to $97 million in interest revenues.[13] On the other hand, project costs were rising from the high inflation of the late 1970s. It can be argued that the District and the Bureau may have saved several million dollars by keeping the project moving. The Bureau of Reclamation maintains that its use of the Water Supply Act was neither imprudent nor illegal and believes it has "an honest difference of opinion" with the General Accounting Office.[14]

The District's use of the Water Supply Act gives a snapshot of typical District policies and operations: the composition of the District's board of directors; the District's interaction with other government agencies, such as the Bureau of Reclamation; the degree of public input into District affairs; and the District's funding procedures and financial responsibilities. These policies and operations are discussed later in this chapter.

District board members usually represent water development interests; board members also feel that completing the CUP is their primary task. This may have encouraged board members to place project completion above financial and project management considerations.[15]

The involvement of the Bureau of Reclamation permitted use of the Water Supply Act, since only the Bureau can invoke this law in connection with a federal project. The District's use of the Water Supply Act allowed construction at Jordanelle to continue while postponing a referendum vote by taxpayers in the District to increase the project's repayment ceiling. This referendum vote was the only direct voice the public had in the operation of the District, and continued construction at this stage of the project may have made a successful referendum vote more likely.

The use of the Water Supply Act also made available federal funding with deferred repayment at an attractive interest rate. In contrast, a cost-sharing arrangement would have required the District to work out its funding in advance of construction, a decidedly less attractive option.

All of these elements of District operations contributed to its use of the Water Supply Act.

Forces Contributing to Increased District Responsiveness

When the District was created, there seemed to be almost unanimous support for the Central Utah Project—the 1965 referendum for the original repayment contract passed by 93 percent.[16] By the 1980s, however, the District became aware that there were exceptions to the perceived general public support for the District and the project. The National Wildlife Federation challenged the District's use of the Water Supply Act, a geologist who had worked with mining companies in the Park City Mining District questioned the safety of the proposed Jordanelle Dam, and individual critics voiced their concerns about the District, the Bureau, and the CUP.

Since then, critics have further questioned the appointment process of the District board and the policies and day-to-day operations of the District and have criticized the Bureau's record of environmental mitigation and CUP management. In addition, the 1992 CUP Completion Act, which authorized the funds needed to complete the project, makes the District responsible for the remaining project construction and requires it to pay planning and construction costs in advance. Each of these challenges has forced changes upon the District and requires it to consider issues other than merely building the CUP.

The District's Appointment Process

During the 1960s and 1970s, CUWCD board members were appointed by the judiciary; citizens interested in serving on the District board petitioned the court for an appointment. Once a director was appointed, continual reappointment was almost assured. This procedure created a low-profile appointment process that allowed a director to sit on the District board for years.

By the early 1980s, some in the water industry began to feel that the District board's judicial appointment process had made it unresponsive to the public it was supposed to represent. The judiciary tended to appoint farmers, ranchers, and other agriculturalists,[17] who are a small percentage of the population in Utah and make only a minor contribution to the state's eco-nomy. Additionally, board members often represented either water providers, such as irrigation companies, or large-scale water users' associations.[18] Critics argued that such a board of directors was unresponsive, did not represent the general public, and gave the board a vested interest in water development.

The Timpanogos Planning and Water Management Agency, an organization representing seven northern Utah County cities, found a total lack of communication and responsiveness between the District and its constituents. The agency claimed that the District had proceeded with designs for a treatment plant and an aqueduct for Utah County, without asking the cities how much water they would actually need from the projects. The agency charged the District with having a "we know best" attitude, and that it could afford to be indifferent to water users who were locked into the CUP through ad valorem taxes.

The Timpanogos Agency tied this lack of responsiveness to the appointment process of the board of directors and questioned the constitutionality of court appointments: "We, along with many others throughout the State, have felt . . . that we have been taxed without representation."[19] Finally, according to Don Christiansen, former chairman of the Timpanogos Agency, the agency felt that the general public was not well represented on the District board.[20]

Another critic of the appointment process was the Utah Water Research Laboratory, a research group affiliated with Utah State University. A UWRL report on water districts claimed that court appointments had created "essentially a self-perpetuating [CUWCD] board of directors with reappointments being perfunctorily made by the district court with little public input and no control by the state."[21] The report noted some common criticisms of a court-appointed board: It lacks broad-based public participation, eliminates the element of compromise, has the potential for imposing a minority will on the general population, and makes a District immune to public pressures.[22]

In response to the previously mentioned forces, the 1983 Utah legislature amended the Water Conservancy Act and changed the District's appointment process. Now each of the nineteen board members is appointed by the governor from three nominations for each vacancy, made by locally elected county commissioners. The state senate confirms these appointments.

The Timpanogos Agency commended the legislature's action, but felt that the District board would still not be fully representative for several years, since directors who had been appointed by the court would remain until they had completed their terms of office. In August 1983 the agency filed suit against the District, challenging the constitutionality of the judicial appointment of water district board members. In October 1984, *Timpanogos Planning and Water Management Agency v. Central Utah Water Conservancy District* came before the Utah Supreme Court. The court declared that the process of judicial appointments violated the separation of powers clause and was unconstitutional. By this time, thirteen District board members had been appointed under the amended Water Conservancy Act. The court declared that the six remaining directors, who were all up for reappointment later in the year, would immediately be removed from their positions and subjected to the new appointment process. When the state legislature finished its deliberations in December, it had confirmed all six of the governor's nominees, four of whom were directors who had been removed from the board two months earlier.[23]

What effect has the change in the appointment process actually had on the composition of the board? A year after the change, Tim R. Miller of the Political Science Department of the University of Utah argued that the District board still leaned toward agricultural interests. He claimed that board members who are leaders of irrigation companies have a vested interest in water development generally and direct or indirect interests in the completion of the Central Utah Project.[24] And a 1989 audit of the District still noted concerns about a lack of public representation (see discussion below).

However, Don Christiansen, the leading force behind the Timpanogos lawsuit and now general manager of the District, believes that the new appointment process has definitely changed the composition and character of the board. He says that the board is now truly representative of the people who elect their county commissioners.[25]

Table 3.1 shows the composition of the District board during 1977, 1983, 1991, and 1992. The table considers the professional backgrounds of board members and includes both past and present affiliations. The information for the 1977 and 1983 boards is more complete than that for the later boards because the District's 1977 and 1983 Annual Reports contain a detailed list of the directors' affiliations.

Table 3.1
Composition of CUWCD Board of Directors

	1977[a]	1983[b]	1991[c]	1992[d]
Farmer/Rancher	10	11	12	12
Canal/Irrigation Company	11	11	6	8
Water Users Association	10	8	6	8
County Commissioner	8	5	2	2
WCD-Affiliated	6	7	6	4
City Government	3	3	3	4
Non-Agricultural Business	2	1	3	4
Public Works/Utilities	1	3	2	3
Engineer	0	2	3	3
Attorney	3	3	0	0
State Government	1	1	0	1

a. Source: 1977 CUWCD *Annual Report*.

b. Source: 1983 CUWCD *Annual Report* (composition of the board just before the change in the appointment process).

c. Source: 1991 CUWCD *Annual Report*, personal resumes, and interviews (one Utah County director's seat vacant).

d. Source: 1992 CUWCD *Annual Report*, personal resumes, and interviews.

The authors' analysis of and experience with the board of directors lead us to believe that the change in the appointment process has not substantially affected the composition of the District board, but has increased the turnover rate of board members. In the court-appointed boards, a majority of members were involved in agriculture, and many members fit several of our categories, forming a kind of interlocking directorate among agriculture, water providers, water users, and water conservancy districts. In the four boards we analyzed, including the governor-appointed 1991 and 1992 boards, we determined that at least ten of the nineteen board members fit the farmer/ rancher category. In the 1991 board, six directors—almost one-third—were affiliated with another water conservancy district. And in our most recent data, four board members fit all three of the Farmer/Rancher, Water Users Association, and Canal/ Irrigation Company categories.

The most significant effect of the new appointment process

has been to increase the turnover rate of board members; the old appointment process could be considered a reappointment process. From the creation of the District in 1964 to the change in the appointment process in 1983, thirty-six individuals served on the District board; from 1983 to 1993, twenty-nine people have served. This amounts to a turnover rate of 1.8 per year for the first twenty years and 2.9 per year since the change in the appointment process. Board members are now more likely to be involved in current local government and thus more aware of the needs and concerns of their constituencies.

If critics were correct in asserting that board members who are stockholders in irrigation companies have a vested interest in water development, then the change in the appointment process has not affected the board's vested interests. However, the presence of this vested interest would not be surprising, since the District was formed to develop Utah's share of Colorado River water. The new appointment process nevertheless increases the likelihood that board members will be responsive to changing public attitudes toward water development.

Changes in the District's Operations

Between 1989 and 1992, the Utah Office of the Legislative Auditor General conducted a series of audits on the state's special districts. The audit of the CUWCD was undertaken in response to several legislators' concerns about it's direction and internal management.[26]

The auditors were concerned that the composition of the board of directors, structured to represent water development interests, had created a District with a narrow mission. Board members tend to believe that the District's most important goal is completing the CUP. According to the audit, this goal can conflict with other public policies, such as economic efficiency.[27] And despite the fact that the board's appointment process had been changed six years earlier, the audit still noted concerns over lack of public representation.[28]

In addition, the auditors found that the District had been accumulating cash reserves without a clearly identified need.

Because the directors did not know precisely when and how much cash would be needed for constructing CUP projects, they had built up its cash reserves and taxed property owners at the maximum rate allowed by law. In the early 1980s the District had used these funds in conjunction with the Water Supply Act to continue construction of the CUP. In 1988 the District had $22.7 million in undesignated cash reserves, which it invested in short-term notes to keep the funds available.

These cash reserves were built primarily through the debt service sinking fund, which was created to pay the District's contractual repayments to the Bureau of Reclamation. However, the audit found that the fund was never used to pay off these debts, since they are paid out of its budgeted expenses each year. A previous external audit in 1985 had concluded that in order to increase public accountability, the board needed to specify the debt service sinking fund's purpose. At the time of the 1989 audit, this recommendation had not been implemented.[29]

The Utah Uniform Fiscal Procedures For Special Districts Act of 1988 limits the total amount of cash reserves that can be accumulated in a district's general fund. Before 1988, the District kept all its cash reserves, including those designated as the debt service sinking fund, in its general fund. However, shortly after the Uniform Fiscal Procedures Act was passed, the District transferred the debt service sinking fund revenues from the general fund to a separate debt service fund. According to the audit, this transfer was made so that the District could avoid the cap on the general fund. The audit concluded that the District had accumulated $11.3 million in funds over the cap set by the Uniform Fiscal Procedures Act.[30]

In 1993 the Legislative Auditor General's Office followed up on the audits conducted between 1989 and 1992. It found that the District had implemented most of the auditors' recommendations, including those for increasing financial responsibility. The District has further increased board oversight of its operations in response to this audit. The debt service sinking fund has been discontinued and its funds moved into the U.S. Obligation Reserve Fund, which is used to make Bonneville Unit repayments. Other accounts such as the Construction Reserve Fund and Emergency Reserve Fund now have defined purposes and written policies for use. All funds have a "cap," or maximum amount, so that once a fund reaches the cap, no further revenues can be allocated to the fund.

The follow-up audit also found that the board still invests funds solely in short-term notes and that the District is still taxing at the maximum allowable rate. However, conditions have changed since the original audit, and the CUP Completion Act requires the District to provide more of the cost of the CUP. According to the follow-up audit, the District needed an estimated $183 million beyond its 1993 operating budget to meet the cost-sharing requirement of the act.[31]

As of 1993, the District had about $23.5 million in cash reserves, half of which were designated for specific projects and the remainder of which were available for the 1993 operating budget.[32] During that year, the District spent about $7 million of its own funds as the local cost share for the studies required by the CUP Completion Act.[33]

Another District change is increased board oversight of financial decisions and Central Utah Project construction. In 1990 the District adopted an Administrative Code that requires a detailed budget process involving board committees in individual department reviews and the full board in a thorough review of the entire budget before the annual public hearing in December. New procurement policies govern the selection of consultants, the awarding of contracts, and the purchase of necessary property, equipment, and materials.[34]

In 1993 the board established the Central Utah Project Completion Act Committee to oversee CUPCA activities and ensure that the CUP will be properly managed. The board meets with this committee to discuss the status of project elements and decisions that will be on the board's formal agenda. The committee requires that detailed information be provided to board members when they make project decisions, such as approving annual consultant work plans and contracting for agency and interest group participation in project planning. Future decisions of this committee will include project construction alternatives, policies for water sales contracts, and local cost-share funding.

Increased District Responsiveness and Responsibility
after the CUP Completion Act

The 1985 supplemental repayment contract authorized the
District to increase its repayment obligation for the municipal
and industrial component of the CUP, but by 1989, federal funds
were running out again. The Utah congressional delegation
introduced a bill to authorize additional funds to complete the
project, but this effort was blocked by California Congressman
George Miller and Senate Majority Leader George Mitchell, who
were intent on reclamation reform. Miller and Mitchell were
concerned in part about the Bureau of Reclamation's record of
poor response to environmental impacts (see chapter nine).

It took over three years to craft a modified CUP Completion
Act that was environmentally acceptable. The District and Utah
Congressman Wayne Owens worked with environmentalists, the Northern Ute Indians, and water users to develop a
mutually acceptable bill that provided cost savings, more local
participation in project management and funding, and greater
attention to the CUP's impact on the environment.

The CUPCA of 1992 is different from any previous water
project bill in that it contains generous funding for water efficiency and conservation, environmental mitigation, and a settlement of water rights claims of the Northern Utes. There is
almost as much funding for these other elements as for actual
CUP project construction: $460.3 million versus $463.5 million.

The act authorizes a cornucopia of non-CUP studies, projects, and funding, including a groundwater study; the Wasatch
County Water Efficiency Project; the Utah Lake Salinity Control
Study; the Provo River Study; the Water Management
Improvement Plan; funds for instream flow, riparian habitat,
wetlands, parkways and recreation, and fish and wildlife; funds
for tribal farming operations; funds for improving reservoirs,
streams, roads, and habitat on the Northern Ute Reservation; the
Tribal Development Fund; and the Utah Reclamation Mitigation
and Conservation Account, which will provide income for environmental mitigation in perpetuity, since only the interest in the
account can be withdrawn.

One interpretation of the District's involvement is that the

board finally recognized that all legitimate interests need
be satisfied in order for the project to proceed. It worked
environmental groups such as the Utah Wildlife Leadership
Coalition, the Stonefly Society of the Wasatch, the Sierra Club,
the Utah Trout Foundation, the National Audubon Society, and
the Salt Lake Fish and Game Association, as well as state
wildlife and water resource agencies, to formulate a project that
would satisfy critics of the Bureau's environmental record.

On the other hand, the District may simply have been forced
to include nontraditional interests in the CUPCA to enable it to
pass. If this is true, then the environmental and other interest
groups were "bought off" by "green pork," and the District's
"openness" toward environmentalists may have been based on
expediency rather than on a genuinely inclusive attitude.

The act transfers the responsibility for completing the CUP
from the Bureau of Reclamation to the District, which is now
responsible for designing and building the project, receiving the
federal authorizations, and setting local cost sharing. The provisions of the CUPCA were intended to ensure that funds appropriated to the CUP would actually be used to complete the project, that the District would maintain a balance between project
construction and environmental concerns, and that the project
would be completed on time and within its authorization.

Congress transferred control of the CUP to the District
because of concerns over some of the Bureau's past management
practices, noting that "Almost since its inception, the Central
Utah Project has been plagued with serious financial and environmental problems."[35] Congress noted that the Bureau has
been criticized repeatedly for mismanagement of the Colorado
River Storage Project cost ceiling. The Bureau had combined the
cost ceiling figures for individual CRSP projects into one figure,
allowing it to "borrow" cost ceiling from inactive projects to
cover cost overruns on active projects. Congress found that such
borrowing had allowed the Bureau to overspend the Bonneville
Unit cost ceiling by $214 million. Furthermore, the Bureau's
practice of assigning unreasonably high overhead expenses had
significantly increased the Bonneville Unit's cost.[36] This increase
in the unit's cost contributed to the previously discussed need to
use the Water Supply Act.

Congress was also concerned with the Bureau's inadequate record of mitigating the CUP's impacts on fish and wildlife. The major environmental impacts of the project have been loss of instream flow in trout streams, destruction of wetlands, loss of riparian habitat, loss of big-game winter range, excessive discharges to natural watercourses, and adverse water quality impacts from irrigation drainage flows. Congress eliminated from the CUPCA two "pump-back" water recirculation schemes the Bureau had proposed for meeting instream flow requirements, saying that these projects were "costly and impractical."[37] In addition, members of Congress believed that the CUP could be completed sooner and more cheaply if the District managed the construction; the District has in fact completed a canal rehabilitation project for substantially less than the Bureau's cost estimates. The congressional report noted that the secretary of the interior would still be able to oversee project spending to safeguard the public interest.[38]

The CUP Completion Act authorizes the funds to complete the CUP, but it requires that the District meet certain conditions before it can use the money. To ensure that there will be sufficient demand for irrigation and drainage water, the CUPCA requires that water users contract for at least 90 percent of the I&D water before the final design can begin. To encourage the District to complete the CUP quickly, the CUPCA terminates the funding for specific CUP components in five years, unless construction has begun.

To make the District more financially responsible, the act requires it to pay 35 percent of CUP planning and construction costs as the federal appropriations are used, rather than repaying the costs over forty years, after the project first delivers water. In other words, the District must now put 35 cents toward each dollar before that dollar can be spent. This money is coming from local taxpayers and the state legislature, so the District is now more accountable to local constituencies.

These requirements have forced the District to become more financially cautious. It uses consultants instead of building a large staff as the Bureau of Reclamation did, and it controls its overhead by paying only for the specific services it needs. The District is careful not to request more federal appropriations than it can effectively use each year, and it involves all interested agencies in developing its annual work plans and objectives.

The District's 1992 *Annual Report* states, "For the first time in the history of water reclamation in the United States, a local state entity has stewardship of a federally funded project to manage construction features and maintain most facilities upon their completion."[39] The secretary of the interior and congressional committees are closely monitoring the District's progress, and if this experiment is successful, the arrangement could become a model for future water projects across the country.

There has also been a demonstrable increase in public involvement in the District's activities. In the past, the general public had little influence on any aspect of the District's operations, including who was appointed to the board,[40] which CUP projects would be built, how the CUP would be funded, and how much residents would be taxed.[41]

In 1985 the District and the Bureau of Reclamation negotiated a second repayment contract to allow construction of the CUP to continue; this contract had to be approved in a referendum by the residents of the District. Although the referendum gave the public its only opportunity for a direct voice in constructing the CUP, the referendum allowed only a "yes" or "no" vote; a "no" vote would have killed the entire project.

The District budgeted $125,000 for promoting passage of the 1985 referendum, in addition to its $100,000 annual budget for public education and information. The private sector contributed $140,000 to a pro-CUP organization called the Water for Utah's Future Committee, which was created by the chairman of the Metropolitan Water District of Salt Lake City and chaired by former Utah governor Scott Matheson.[42] This committee did not include CUWCD board members or staff, but the District did provide assistance at the Committee's request.

The District used its budget for literature, pamphlets, and the services of its usual public relations firm. The Water for Utah's Future Committee used its campaign funds for TV commercials, public opinion polls, travel for District speakers (including Don Christiansen and Edward Clyde), and for public relations firms, campaign consultants, and advertising services.

The CUP has always been supported by a majority of Utahns, but it also has been consistently opposed by a vocal minority. While the pro-CUP forces created the Water for Utah's Future Committee, the opposition groups organized the CUP Information Campaign. However, opposition had no established institution, such as the CUWCD, or ready funds, such as the District's budget for public education, with which to make its views heard. Instead, the CUP Information Campaign relied on door-to-door stumping and free media coverage. Perhaps the most visible CUP opponent during this time was University of Utah economist Jon Miller, whose views were publicized in several newspaper articles before the referendum. In one article, Dr. Miller urged voters to reject the supplemental repayment contract, because additional project construction would result in "exorbitant" water costs.[43]

Dr. Miller and the opposition groups took on the formidable task of swinging public opinion away from the project; the District's strategy was to shore up existing support and prevent any anti-CUP environmental or tax reform group from gaining ground. In general, the District did not need to convince voters to change their position, since most voters had traditionally supported the project. Prior to the referendum the public had virtually no voice in the operation of the District or the construction of the CUP; in 1985 the District used taxpayers' own money to try to influence the one direct decision they could make. The referendum passed by a vote of 73 percent in favor.

The public education and information account used in the 1985 referendum does not exist in the budget today. There is an account for public affairs that has a detailed list of work objectives used to justify the budget amount each year. This document is available for public inspection as part of the new budget review and adoption procedures of the District.

The Timpanogos Planning and Water Management Agency had complained about the District's "we know best" attitude when determining cities' future water needs. The CUP Completion Act requires the District to include all interested agencies in its planning. The District now assists local agencies, such as Duchesne City, Provo, Orem, Timpanogos, and the Strawberry Water Users Association, with planning for future growth and invites them to participate in an open planning process.

The CUP Completion Act made the District a federal agency for purposes of completing the CUP, which means that it must comply with the provisions of the National Environmental Policy Act (NEPA). The NEPA process will involve many agencies and groups in CUP construction, including the Utah Division of Wildlife Resources, the U.S. Fish and Wildlife Service, the Bureau of Indian Affairs, the Northern Ute Indian Tribe, the Environmental Protection Agency, the Army Corps of Engineers, and the Natural Resource Conservation Service. The District plans to ensure that these groups participate in its planning process by paying the staff and travel expenses for the representatives of state and federal resource agencies and environmental interest groups who attend District meetings.

Recommended Changes in CUP Funding

In 1993 shortly after the passage of the CUP Completion Act, Governor Mike Leavitt of Utah organized a task force to recommend funding alternatives for the District's share of the CUP. The Central Utah Project Funding Task Force heard testimony primarily from water users, water conservancy districts, and private citizens. Brad Barber, a staff member on the task force, states that this testimony forced a change in the way the District does business. The testimony influenced the task force to recommend that the state not raise taxes to pay for the CUP. Now the District will have to find other ways to finance it, including bonding for some capital projects and "tightening the belt."[44]

According to proponents, bonding would free up other District cash reserves. The District has planned and budgeted to replace the Olmsted Diversion Structure in the Provo River, in order to provide M&I water to Salt Lake and Utah counties. It has also accumulated cash reserves for completing terminal reservoir storage on the Jordan Aqueduct in Salt Lake County. If the District elects to bond for these projects, the cash reserves can be used for CUPCA planning work. The District can "tighten its belt" by not accumulating cash reserves and by deferring additional capital expenditures—thus passing some projects on to customer agencies—until CUPCA planning is completed.

Conclusion

This chapter has discussed fundamental changes that increased the responsiveness of the Central Utah Water Conservancy District. The authors believe that these changes are primarily the result of three forces: judicial decisions, criticism from academics, and political changes in other government entities.

The lawsuit brought by the Timpanogos Water Planning and Management Agency led the Utah Supreme Court to rule that the judicial appointment of District board members was unconstitutional. At the time of the lawsuit, the appointment process had already been changed by the state legislature, but the lawsuit ensured that all current board members were appointed under the new process. The impending lawsuit may well have influenced the legislature to act when it did.

Research by the Utah Water Research Laboratory and Professor Jon Miller provided an alternate perspective on District policies and interests. Academic studies rarely have a direct influence on a district's operations, but they can affect public opinion if their conclusions are publicized by the press. In addition, academic studies are sometimes analyzed by legislative committees.

Government agencies and other bodies can force changes in a special district by amending the acts and regulations that govern its operations. In the case of the CUWCD, changes were initiated by the state legislature, the state legislative auditor general, a governor-appointed task force, and the Congress.

Citizens who were concerned about the District's direction and its management of the CUP gained the attention of the state legislature, which acted in two ways to change the way the District operates. First, the legislature changed the appointment process for district directors to include locally elected officials. Second, the legislature requested an audit by the Utah Office of the Legislative Auditor General to answer legislators' questions about the District's financial management.

The Central Utah Project Funding Task Force, which heard testimony from water users and private citizens, recommended that the state not raise taxes to pay for the District's share of the CUP. This recommendation should cause the District to use its funds wisely. Also, since the District now obtains more project funding from local taxpayers and the state legislature, it must be more accountable to local constituencies.

In 1992, Congress approved the CUP Completion Act, which allows the District to manage the CUP, provided that it complies with NEPA requirements for full public involvement in project planning. This provision, along with the CUPCA's generous funding for environmental mitigation, water conservation, and Native American water rights claims, was a direct result of interest group pressure on the District, state officials, and Congress.

The pressure on the judiciary, the state legislature, and Congress to change the operation and focus of the District was a manifestation of the public's changing attitude toward water development. The public now demands that water policy consider issues such as lifestyle, instream flow, wildlife, the environment, recreation, social justice, and financial responsibility in addition to the traditional concerns of agriculture and urban development.

In 1965 the public's mandate to the District was simply to build the Central Utah Project. In the 1990s the mandate is to complete the project while enhancing Utah's quality of life.

Notes

1. "1962: The Start of Completion," *Colorado River News Report*, December 1962, p. 3.
2. Utah Office of the Legislative Auditor General, *A Performance Audit of the Central Utah Water Conservancy District*, Utah Legislature Report 89-12 (Salt Lake City, 1989), p. 5.
3. United States General Accounting Office, "Bureau of Reclamation's Bonneville Unit: Future Repayment Arrangements," GAO/RCED-86-103 (Washington, D.C., 1986), p. 2. In Committee on Interior and Insular Affairs, *Supplemental Repayment Contract for the Bonneville Unit, Central Utah Project*, 99th Congress, 2nd Session, House Document 58 (Washington, D.C., 1986, pp. 73–83.

4. U.S.GAO, "Future Repayment Arrangements," p. 3.

5. Edward W. Clyde, letter to Don A. Christiansen, March 5, 1986, in Committee on Interior and Insular Affairs, *Supplemental Repayment Contract*, p. 104.

6. The Utah Office of the Legislative Auditor General (*Performance Audit*, p. 8) believes that this cash advance cost the District between $4.8 and $6.4 million in lost interest.

7. U.S.GAO, "Future Repayment Arrangements," p. 4.

8. Ibid., pp. 4–5.

9. Committee on Interior and Insular Affairs, *Supplemental Repayment Contract*, p. 106.

10. Jordanelle's water supply has been increased by 20,000 acre-feet, although this design change occurred around 1967, fourteen years before the Bureau invoked the Water Supply Act. A 1987 CUP report states that Jordanelle's M&I water supply was increased to "provide more efficient use of local [water] supplies" (U.S. Bureau of Reclamation, Upper Colorado Region, *Central Utah Project, Bonneville Unit—Utah: Supplement to Definite Plan Report*, rev. October 1987, p. 33). Even if this design change were related to the Water Supply Act, a claim not made in the report, the District could have deferred the cost of only 20,000 acre-feet, not 60,000, according to the GAO's interpretation.

11. Committee on Interior and Insular Affairs, *Supplemental Repayment Contract*, p. 107.

12. Francis Fericks, "CUP Clashes Flare Again," *Utah Waterline*, May 9, 1984, pp. 1, 12.

13. U.S.GAO, "Future Repayment Arrangements," p. 5.

14. Committee on Interior and Insular Affairs, *Supplemental Repayment Contract*, p. 50.

15. Utah Office of the Legislative Auditor Gerneral, *Performance Audit*, p. 5.

16. "Utah Approves Water Pact by 13-1 Ratio," *Salt Lake Tribune*, December 15, 1965.

17. Utah Office of the Legislative Auditor General, *Performance Audit*, p. 12.

18. Ibid., pp. i–ii.

19. Don A. Christiansen, letter to Jay M. Bagley, August 8, 1983, in Utah Water Research Laboratory, *Impediments to Effective Interactions between Multipurpose Water Districts and Other Governmental Institutions in Urbanizing Areas*, NTIS # PB8 4 125 152 (Logan, Utah: Utah State University, 1983), pp. 110–11.

20. Don A. Christiansen, telephone interview, December 12, 1990.

21. "Study Didn't Oppose CUP, Cazier Says," *Deseret News*, November 13–14, 1985, p. A-15.

22. UWRL, *Impediments*, pp. 61–62.

23. "Brown, Garrett, Lee, Novak, Siddoway, White Get CUP Nod," *Utah Waterline*, December 19, 1984, p. W2.

24. Tim R. Miller, "Politics of the Carter Administration's Hit List Water Initiative: Assessing the Significance of Subsystems in Water Politics" (Ph.D. dissertation, University of Utah, 1984), p. 232.

25. Don A. Christiansen, telephone interview, December 12, 1990.

26. Utah Office of the Legislative Auditor General, *Performance Audit*, p. 3.

27. Ibid., p. 5.

28. Ibid., pp. 3, 12.

29. Ibid., pp. 42–45.

30. Ibid., p. 47.

31. Utah Office of the Legislative Auditor General, *Special Districts Follow-up*, ILR 93-F, March 29, 1993, pp. 7–12.

32. Central Utah Water Conservancy District, *Annual Report*, (Orem, Utah, 1993).

33. Stan Weaver, Central Utah Water Conservancy District comptroller, personal communication, March 1994.

34. Central Utah Water Conservancy District Administrative Code, chapter V, "Financial Matters" and chapter VIII, "Procurement" (Orem, Utah, 1990).

35. Committee on Energy and Natural Resources, United States Senate, *Reclamation Projects Authorization and Adjustment Act of 1992*, Report 102-267 (Washington, D.C., 1992), p. 99.

36. Ibid., pp. 99–100.

37. Ibid., p. 101.

38. Ibid., p. 107.

39. Central Utah Water Conservancy District, *Annual Report* (Salt Lake City, 1992), p. 1.

40. While the district technically has a "citizen board," certain types of citizens, namely farmers, ranchers, large-scale water users, and members of other water districts are overrepresented. Usually several board members are officials in city or county government.

41. While the public has had little direct influence on District affairs, it has had access to information on District operations. The public has always been able to review budget documents and attend the committee and formal board meetings. However, the Utah public rarely avails itself of these opportunities.

42. *Deseret News*, November 8, 1985, p. B-2; Nick Sefakis, minutes of the 486th meeting of the Metropolitan Water District of Salt Lake City, December 30, 1985, p. 73.

43. "Opponent Predicts CUP to Create 'Real Water Crisis'," *Salt Lake Tribune*, September 19, 1985, p. C-2. See also Jon R. Miller and Daniel Underwood, "Distributional Issues in Western Municipal and Industrial Water Supply," *Water Resources Bulletin* 19 (August 1983): 631–40; Jon R. Miller, "On the Behavior of Western Water Agencies under Stress: Renegotiating the Bonneville Unit of the Central Utah Project," Working Paper #85-1, Center for Public Affairs and Administration, Division of Social Science Research, University of Utah (Salt Lake City, January 1985).

44. Brad Barber, telephone interview, February 1, 1994.

CHAPTER FOUR

Water Resources and Tourism

Roy Ramthun

Disputes over water rights are a tradition in the western states. Typically, these disputes have been among ranchers, farmers, the mining industry, the electric power industry, and cities that need water for growing populations. Now a new water user is beginning to take an interest in the management of water resources. The tourism industry, which some experts believe will be the largest industry in the world in a few decades, sees water as one of the strongest attractions bringing vacation travelers to a community.[1] Sometimes this view creates conflicts between communities seeking economic opportunities and other local citizens who prefer to see public resources managed in a less commercial fashion. This chapter examines the tourism industry's stake in water project development and conflicts over development of water recreation facilities at the site of the Jordanelle Reservoir.

Growth of the Tourism Industry

Over the past two decades, the economic base of the state of Utah has changed dramatically. Agriculture and mining no longer employ large numbers of people; by 1993 only 3 percent of the work force was employed in agriculture, with only 1 percent in mining.[2] With the decline of the traditional industries, tourism is now the largest industry in the state of Utah. Travel and tourism-related businesses generate more jobs and revenue than all others combined.[3] With five national parks, six national monuments, and eleven destination ski areas, Utah offers abundant opportunities for travelers. The 1994 *Annual Economic Report to the Governor* states that "Utah's tourism industry is expected to continue to be one of the fastest growing segments of the state's economy."[4] The rural areas of Utah that have traditionally depended on extractive industries are suffering economically, but the small communities located near tourist destinations are growing and thriving.

A tourism destination usually consists of an attraction plus a set of amenities. Often the attraction that draws visitors to an area is part of the public estate, as is the case with national or state parks, national forests, or a large reservoir. The term "commercial amenities" refers to the restaurants, hotels, gift shops, and other service-oriented businesses that make up the tourism industry. These enterprises are highly dependent on a public resource over which they have no direct control. Resource management decisions that might encourage (or discourage) visitors are of tremendous importance to the local businesses; that they have little direct control over the resource has been a point of long-standing frustration .[5]

The Jordanelle Project

As part of the Central Utah Project, the U.S. Bureau of Reclamation and the Central Utah Water Conservancy District have constructed a dam on the Provo River upstream of Heber City, in northern Utah. When filled, the Jordanelle Reservoir will inundate two steep, narrow valleys. The steep banks and depth of these valleys will enable the Jordanelle to store almost twice as much water as the nearby Deer Creek Reservoir, while having only 25 percent more surface area.

These valleys extend north and east from the dam site. The north arm of the reservoir slopes upward through gently rolling terrain. The surrounding vegetation is mostly sagebrush, with stands of aspen, maple, and oak growing along small creeks that drain into the reservoir basin. The east arm of the reservoir reaches into an area known as the West Hills. This is steeper ground, with cliffs and tall rock pinnacles bordering the basin.

The land to the north of this arm supports sagebrush, scrub oak, and some aspen and conifers. The land located between the two arms of the reservoir was acquired to provide winter range for a large herd of mule deer. There are also several golden eagle nesting sites in the area, as well as habitat and breeding grounds for sage grouse.[6]

In conjunction with the construction of the dam and reservoir, the Utah Division of Parks and Recreation has planned a new state park at the site. Jordanelle State Park is currently being developed as a high-quality facility to serve as a model for other water-based recreation facilities in Utah and across the Southwest.[7] Located near the Wasatch Front, this park will help meet the demands of Utah residents for water-based recreation. The park will be designed and operated by the Utah Division of Parks and Recreation; it was always assumed that funding for the construction of the park would be provided by the Bureau. Funding for recreational development does not have to be repaid to the federal government; under section 8 of the Colorado River Storage Project Act, money invested for recreation, fish, and wildlife is considered to be economic development assistance to the state and requires no federal cost sharing.[8]

The Need for Recreational Facilities

Sixty-five percent of Utah's 1,866,000 people live along the Wasatch Front. This area runs for approximately 100 miles through a set of wide valleys in the north-central part of the state and contains the cities of Salt Lake, Ogden, and Provo. It also contains many growing suburban communities.[9]

Utah also has one of the youngest populations in the United States, with a median age in 1990 of only 25 years.[10] Not only is Utah's population young, it is also active. Sports and outdoor activities are highly valued and actively promoted in Utah, where many residents are introduced to fishing, boating, camping, and hunting at early ages.

This active, young population, concentrated in a small portion of the state, has created a high level of demand for all types of recreation facilities. In particular, there is demand for water-based recreation.[11] There are currently six state parks along the

Wasatch Front offering water-based recreation, and all of them have been operating at capacity since the early 1980s. These parks average between 200,000 and 350,000 visitors per year. Because they focus on water-based activities, the majority of visitor use occurs between June and September. Research has shown that the resident market is underserved in most of the facilities associated with water-based recreation.[12] As another indicator of the demand for water-based recreation, a new state park at Jordanelle is expected to receive as many as 5,000 visitors per day during the peak season, with a yearly total of up to 450,000 visitors. Eighty percent of those visitors are expected to be Utah residents.[13]

The demand for recreational facilities is not created solely by Utah residents. The majority of out-of-state visitors who fuel Utah's large commercial recreation and tourism industry come for the outdoor recreation opportunities. While most of these visitors come during the warm-weather months, the state is also known as a center for winter recreation; there are nine ski resorts along the Wasatch Front. After the severe layoffs by the mining industry in the early 1980s, the ski industry is now Utah's largest.[14] The ski resorts and adjacent hotels, restaurants, and other amenities create thousands of jobs, but only on a seasonal basis; the local ski and hospitality industry has a layoff rate of approximately 50 percent during the summer months.[15] Owners and managers of Wasatch Front hospitality and recreation businesses actively seek summer tourism activities, such as boating or fishing, to increase their profits and decrease the seasonality of their industry.

While the demand for water-based recreation is created by both residents and visitors, the two groups are actually very different. Residents participate in simple, family-oriented outdoor activities, while visitors prefer a wider range of activities. Residents tend to utilize rustic facilities, while the visitors enjoy facilities with a "high degree of finish."[16] Visitors also prefer recreation sites with a variety of amenities such as restaurants, gift shops, hotels, and non resource-oriented activities (tennis courts, bars, arcades).[17] There is also a significant difference between how much money out-of-state visitors and Utah residents are willing to pay for recreation. Residents, often young and with families, average $13.50 worth of expenditures per person per day at recreation sites. Nonresident visitors will pay over twice as much, averaging $29.50 per person per day.[18]

Planning Recreational Facilities

The Jordanelle site has been identified as a reservoir location since the beginning of the Central Utah Project. Almost all southwestern reservoirs support recreation facilities, and there was never any reason to believe this one would be different. Preliminary planning for a state park began in the early 1970s. The National Environmental Policy Act requires that an environmental impact statement (EIS) be completed for federally funded projects that affect the environment; the EIS for recreation development at the site was completed in 1978. Bruce Maw, the project leader for the Jordanelle master plan, noted that this statement set limits on which areas of the site could be developed. It identified areas of "critical" wildlife habitat that must be protected, effectively prohibiting development in many parts of the proposed park and it also set limits on how many sites could be developed in those areas of the park left open to development.

Information from the EIS was largely unused until 1989, when actual planning for the recreation facilities began. This long delay was due to the construction schedule of the various reservoirs and facilities that comprise the Central Utah Project. The Jordanelle dam was completed a year ahead of schedule, in October 1992, and the reservoir is expected to fill by 1996. The Bureau acquired the land for the reservoir plus additional land to provide a "buffer zone" above the high-water line, intended to protect the reservoir from the effects of adjacent development, mitigate impacts on wildlife, provide flood control, maintain water quality, and provide recreation opportunities. In all, the reservoir will have 3,000 acres of water surface and 4,000 acres of adjoining land when the reservoir is full.[19] However, only 968 acres are available for development, primarily on the west side of the reservoir; the EIS requires most of the land to be used for wildlife habitat.

Planning the recreation facilities was the responsibility of the state's Division of Parks and Recreation, with the support of the Bureau. Because this was a federally funded project, federal guidelines called for public involvement in the planning process. The state and the Bureau contracted with a multidisciplinary design team headed by Bingham Engineering of Salt Lake City to help draft the plan. The design team consisted of land-use planners, engineers, an economic research group, liability lawyers, and a marina design company. The process involved the following:

1. a random-sample survey of residents in the six Wasatch Front counties.

2. a series of "scoping" meetings in which members of the public could provide initial input.

3. development of an "interim report" containing alternative plans using the input received at the scoping meetings.

4. a second round of public hearings to evaluate the proposed alternatives.

5. team review of public comments and modification of the selected alternative.

6. final public review.

7. State Parks Board approval.

8. commissioning an engineering firm to prepare design specifications.

Public involvement, mandated by the National Environmental Policy Act and state planning guidelines, is used frequently and often provides a forum for interests that may not otherwise have access to policymakers. In the case of the Jordanelle development, this planning procedure led to heated debate and discussion of politically complex issues. It became what one of the participants called "a morass."

Public Survey Results

The initial public opinion survey of Wasatch Front residents was designed and analyzed by Professors Gary Ellis and Taylor Ellis of the University of Utah's Department of Recreation and Leisure. The survey was administered as a random-sample telephone questionnaire by Dan Jones and Associates of Salt Lake City. Along with a standardized set of questions, this survey included an open-ended qualitative question. It asked the sampled residents their opinion regarding the proposed Jordanelle park.

The results of this survey showed clearly that Wasatch Front residents were in favor of a new state park close to the cities. They were also in favor of a park that would cost only a modest amount to visit, provide simple but clean facilities, and not diminish local wildlife populations. The responses to the open-ended opinion question were often quite explicit. A majority of responses expressed the opinion that the facility should not be overly developed, commercialized, or expensive.[20] "From the resident surveys, the overwhelming desire is for facilities which are basic (albeit high quality) but that commercial recreation and artificial recreational opportunities be limited."[21] This survey was good news for Utah Division of Parks and Recreation; the general public preferred the type of facility that the UDPR has traditionally operated.[22] Bruce Maw of Bingham Engineering added that the UDPR, with limited funding and manpower, would prefer to construct a park that would not be difficult to manage or maintain.[23] The EIS had established a limited scope for development at Jordanelle, with wildlife habitat protection a priority for the facility; the public's preferences dovetailed nicely with the preferences of both the EIS and the UDPR.

Results of the Public Meetings

The input received by state and federal planners in the scoping meetings differed dramatically from the survey results. These were designed to gather public input about certain aspects of the park before drawing up the preliminary plans and were attended primarily by representatives of the Wasatch and Summit county governments and private businessmen from the local area. While the park is actually located in Wasatch County, it is also very close to the ski resort community of Park City, which is in Summit County. The representatives of these counties had a number of concerns about the new development, but two issues were brought up repeatedly: the quality of the facilities and the extent of the development.

Representatives of the counties viewed the new facility as a tremendous asset to the local economy. Local governments in both counties had decided prior to the beginning of the public involvement phase that they would do everything possible to ensure that the state planned a facility that would meet their needs. Park City in particular, with an economy built on tourism, saw a water-based recreation facility as a way to draw summer visitors and "round out" their seasonal industry. According to Bob Mathis, county planner for Wasatch County and a member of the task force formed by the two counties, "We were concerned that the planners would rely heavily on the results of the public survey, which didn't represent the needs and desires of non-resident visitors. We wanted some well-built, imaginative facilities. We didn't want to see the state build another boat-camp."[24]

Both Mathis and Jennifer Harrington, a planning specialist for Park City, claimed that the UDPR was not ready to accept the counties' input. Bob Mathis stated that the hearing process "got away from the DPR. They asked for input and got a lot of input they didn't like."[25] Jennifer Harrington argued that "the parks people were not ready to accept the public input process. They'll probably find some way to throw this plan out the window yet."[26] However, the UDPR viewed the issue from a different perspective: they saw it as balancing the preferences of the public against the demands of a few private interests.

The people representing Wasatch and Summit counties realized their concerns were similar and decided to form the Wasatch-Summit Joint Task Force to present a united front when making their wishes known to state and federal planners. Some individuals from these counties had actively prepared for the public hearings for as much as a year in advance. Private citizens spent their own funds making preparations. Visits were made to other reservoirs and parks to view the types of facilities that were available.[27] Much of this preparation anticipated potential concession contracts.

The Local Issues

The public hearing process went on from June through September of 1989. The issues that were raised in regard to the development of the Jordanelle State Park are not exclusive to that facility; other parks have experienced similar conflicts. Four basic issues emerged during the planning process: quality of facilities, concessions, control of water surfaces, and difficulty of compromise.

Quality of Facilities

The issue of quality is one area in which the residents and representatives of the nonresident market agreed. Even residents with a strong camping orientation preferred flush-toilet facilities and modified campsites. Task force members continually pointed out the necessity of high-quality construction coupled with prompt and regular maintenance to create an attractive facility. The task force members, however, were generally in favor of a much larger number of facilities.

Concessions

The extent of concessionaire involvement in the planning process was a critical issue. Many of the individuals who attended the public hearings were actively involved in pursuing concession contracts: some produced estimates that concessions at Jordanelle could produce annual revenues of $1.5 million. Much of the discussion was focused on the extent to which concessions would be developed.

The UDPR had been uncomfortable with the scale of the development since the beginning of the project, feeling that their manpower and budget would be drained attempting to manage a highly developed and heavily used facility. The counterargument from the private sector was to contract the construction and maintenance of facilities such as the marina, yacht club, and a hotel to private business. In this type of arrangement, the private businesses would build the facilities and subsequently operate them on a for-profit basis.

In the opinion of Fred Liljegren, the Bureau's representative at the hearings, the Utah UDPR has not had much experience in dealing with large-scale concessionaires, and the relationship has often been problematic.[28] If a private company contracts to provide a service and then cannot meet its obligations, the responsibility of providing that service and finding a replacement concessionaire falls to the UDPR.

Some compromises have been made on this issue, however. In the original plan private firms were encouraged to develop an eighteen-hole golf course, but this idea did not prove practical and was dropped from the final plan. In addition, some entrepreneurs suggested that a three- to four-hundred slip marina would be more appropriate than the seventy-five slip marina planned by the UDPR. However, the division's plan was based on extensive studies of marina use, both locally and nationally, by the Jordanelle Design Team; they determined that only seventy-five slips could be justified.

Currently, the UDPR is developing an "extremely aggressive and complex private concessionaire prospectus," designed to improve the coordination of public and private activities in the park.[29]

Control of Water Surfaces

There was a great deal of discussion at the hearings regarding the management of water activities. When a wide variety of water-based activities are allowed on a small body of water at the same time, conflicts between the participants usually occur. The needs and desires of fishermen are very different from those of water-skiers, windsurfers, or jetskiers. All of these user groups utilize water surfaces differently, and the proximity of an incompatible activity can affect the enjoyment and sometimes even the safety of a recreational user.

Judging from the results of the public survey, many members of the public felt that too many activities were being planned for one facility, but no decision was made by the UDPR or the task force to ask for limits on uses until the project was in the final design phase. At many smaller reservoirs, restrictions are placed on some of these activities, particularly on high-speed motorized uses. There may be horsepower restrictions on motorboats that effectively limit speeds, or there may be restrictions on times when an activity is permitted. At Jordanelle, the plan originally called for the lake to be "zoned" into areas for high-speed and for low-speed activities. Previous studies of recreational behavior have shown, however, that boaters seldom recognize these types of boundaries.[30] Thus the zoning plan would require extensive enforcement.[31] One UDPR official, speaking at a meeting in October of 1990, called the Jordanelle "a management nightmare" because of the manpower and enforcement requirements of the water zoning. In 1994 an administrative decision was made to omit water zoning from the plan.[32]

The Difficulty of Compromise

Compromise between the desire of state residents for a rustic facility and the tourism industry's preference for extensive development and heavy usage is difficult. Exclusive of mitigation lands, Jordanelle has only 968 acres available for development; there is not much potential for separation of incompatible activities and facilities. Despite these difficulties, Jordanelle State Park is quickly becoming a reality:

> Major facilities such as the Rock Cliff nature center, the regional office and maintenance complex, group pavilions, marina amenities at Hailstone and recreation convenience structures, such as rest rooms, camp service centers and picnic shelters can all be seen rising above the horizon.[33]

Rock Cliff, one of the park's two recreation areas, opened in 1994; the other area, Hailstone, is scheduled to open in 1995.

Conclusion

Water-based recreation in the Southwest is a major financial asset. Water sports areas in this arid region of the country draw large numbers of people, both from the local area and from a larger regional market. From the point of view of business, a minimally developed reservoir is good, but a reservoir that attracts free-spending vacation travelers is even better. In many small western communities, the tourism industry is often the only viable industry left.

A tourism destination usually consists of an attraction and a set of amenities, generally many small businesses that are dependent on the flow of people to the attraction.[34] In the Jordanelle case, much of the debate has been due to the tourism industry's efforts to gain some control over the development and management of a state-owned resource. In other words, private interests have attempted to exert control over public resources, in an effort to increase their potential profits.[35]

In Utah, the agency that develops and operates state-owned recreation sites is the Division of Parks and Recreation. The UDPR's mission, as defined by the state legislature, is to be "the authority on parks and recreation within the state."[36] The Legislature provides very few specific guidelines for the managers of the state's forty-seven parks, although there are some suggestions that the DPR should protect wildlife and the natural environment, encourage use of its facilities, and promote the state's tourism industry. Unfortunately, these suggestions do not represent priorities; there are no general guidelines for situations where these goals are in conflict. Nevertheless, the division has developed rules for most parks that articulate unique priorities. Terry Green of UDPR notes that each park is unique, and management priorities are determined by site conditions, resource qualities, and park mission statements.[37]

In the 1800s Americans saw their land falling under private ownership or being depleted of resources for the sake of industry. They responded, through their governments, by setting aside parcels that would be maintained in a natural state for the public's use and enjoyment. The operations of most park and recreation management agencies since that time have been guided by the lofty goal of serving the public good.

Today this management philosophy is being questioned, particularly by those who have a financial stake in the issue. According to Fred Liljegren of the Bureau, officials familiar with the public involvement process know that it attracts people with special interests, while the general public remains largely uninvolved.[38] Bruce Maw met individually with the representatives of forty potentially affected interest groups, including the Stonefly Society (a fly-fishing group), Bicycle Utah, the Wasatch Mountain Club, and the Utah Travel Council, as well as inviting them to the public hearings. "We had very little response from them. A few may have sent letters. Many individuals with commercial interests became involved with the county task forces, but the other interest groups really did not participate in the planning process. . . . The poll taken by the university did show some support for a smaller, less developed facility, but there were few people attending the hearing that voiced that opinion. The commercial interests were well represented but other interest groups stayed away."[39]

While public involvement and open debate appear to be ideal tools for planning resource allocation within a democracy, there are limitations to this system. In California's Yosemite National Park, where concession revenues top $84 million per year, the concessionaire conducted its own survey, mailing out tens of thousands of brochures advising patrons to oppose Park Service plans to scale back concession development.[40] Opposition to development schemes is usually by individual citizens and local environmental groups who lack the sophisticated persuasion techniques and money available to commercial interests.

Politicians are often in favor of commercial development in parks, especially if they receive substantial campaign donations from commercial interests. Alston Chase, in his book *Playing God in Yellowstone*, discusses reasons why elected representatives will support even poorly planned or environmentally unsound development. Construction and development provide jobs, divert cash into local businesses, and increase the tax base. Politicians who bring prosperity to their districts are more likely to be reelected; this creates an incentive to overlook long-term resource management policy in favor of short-term economic benefits.[41] Because all resource management agencies are ultimately accountable to some elected body, the opinions of legislators will eventually have an effect upon management decisions. It is not surprising that these factors may create a situation where our recreation resources are managed by local special interest groups instead of professional managers.

This conclusion has a number of implications for public officials responsible for planning, developing, and managing water-based recreation facilities. The first is that they must understand that the public hearing process opens the floor to many factions, including those who want to use a recreation facility and those who want to augment their business. These and other factions may each have legitimate claims and concerns; and they may not be inclined to compromise or even to admit the legitimacy of other views. At the same time, none of these groups may represent the concerns of the general public that, as a whole, pays for the operation of these facilities with their taxes. Resource managers must anticipate controversy and special interest involvement with new projects of significant size.

A second point to remember is that the public hearing process is here to stay. Planning a major development through this kind of "committee approach" requires skills that are traditional to architects, engineers, and land-use planners. Skills in public education and public relations, as well as in group facilitation or negotiation, will be useful to officials trying to bring a variety of viewpoints together on common ground.

The priorities of managing agencies must be clarified and stated. An agency's mission as it regards resource protection, tourism, and development is a vital factor in the planning of new construction. If these objectives are not spelled out, then there are no criteria for decision making. In the Jordanelle case, the Utah legislature made important decisions as to the role of the Division of Parks and Recreation; some of these decisions contradicted other planning tools, including the public opinion survey, the State Comprehensive Outdoor Recreation Plan process, and hearings. The managers who make development decisions must often work out compromise plans that take into account these conflicting forms of input.

Finally, it must be recognized that the tourism industry is growing and that it has a financial stake in resource decisions. To professionals in the parks division this is obvious, but legislators, interest groups, and the public are often less willing to concede this point. Resource management agencies have worked with traditional industries such as agriculture and timber for decades and have reached some understanding regarding the use of public resources. This type of long-term relationship should also be developed between tourism industry representatives and resource managers. For this to happen, however, the vast collection of small businesses that comprise the tourism industry must become more organized and then develop a partnership with resource planners.

This sort of process is not a pipe dream. Through the use of high-profile commissions and public hearings, several states have put together long-range tourism development policies. Florida, Michigan, and New Mexico are states where tourism businesses have been able to clarify their objectives and develop good working relations with resource agencies. In these cases, both sides are willing to make compromises so that public parks and tourism facilities complement each other without adversely affecting the resource on which they all depend.[42] Perhaps Jordanelle State Park can become a model for this kind of planning in Utah.

Notes

1. This predominance is especially striking if the concept of tourism is expanded to include the "leisure" industry, which includes all forms of entertainment and recreation.

2. Utah Office of Planning and Budget, *Annual Economic Report to the Governor* (Salt Lake City, 1994), p. 44.

3. Paul Rolly, "Utah's Urban Economic Growth Belies State's Rural Depression," *Salt Lake Tribune,* August 11, 1991, pp. 1, 2.

4. Utah Office of Planning and Budget, *Annual Economic Report to the Governor* (Salt Lake City, 1994), p. 162. Also see Utah Office of Planning and Budget, the Utah Department of Community and Economic Development, and the Bureau of Economic and Business Research at the University of Utah, "EDA Tourism Study," working draft (Salt Lake City, 1991).

5. Uel Blank, *The Community Tourism Imperative* (State College, Penn.: Venture Publishing, 1989), p. 99–105, 175–181.

6. U.S. Bureau of Reclamation and Utah Division of Parks and Recreation (UDPR), *Jordanelle State Park Master Plan Final Report and Technical Data* (Salt Lake City, 1985).

7. Ibid.

8. Fred Liljegren, interview, November 20, 1990.

9. Utah Office of Planning and Budget, *Annual Economic Report to the Governor* (Salt Lake City, 1994), p. 73.

10. Ibid., p. 32.

11. See Utah Division of Parks and Recreation, *1992 Utah State Comprehensive Outdoor Recreation Plan* (SCORP), (Salt Lake City, 1993), pp. 163, 166, 214.

12. Economic Research Associates, *Memorandum to Jordanelle Planning Team* (San Francisco: Economic Research Associates), 1989.

13. U.S. Bureau of Reclamation and UDPR, *Jordanelle State Park Master Plan,* p. 26.

14. Economic Research Associates, *Memorandum to Jordanelle Planning Team,* p. 1.

15. John Crossley, interview, November 25, 1990.

16. In a recent survey, resident tourists listed "scenery" and "being in a natural environment" as the most enjoyable part of a vacation. University of Utah Survey Research Center, *Utah Consumer Survey* (Salt Lake City, January 1994), p. 56.

17. John Crossley, interview, November 25, 1990.

18. U.S. Bureau of Reclamation, Utah Projects Office (Salt Lake City, 1989).

19. U.S. Bureau of Reclamation and UDPR, *Jordanelle State Park Master Plan.*

20. Gary D. Ellis and Taylor E. Ellis, "Public Opinion Survey in Support of the Jordanelle Planning Process," unpublished research, Department of Recreation and Leisure (University of Utah, 1989).

21. U.S. Bureau of Reclamation, *Jordanelle State Park Master Plan.*

22. Terry Green, interviews, November 1 and 14, 1990.

23. Bruce Maw, interview, November 16, 1990.

24. Bob Mathis, interview, November 14, 1990.

25. Ibid.

26. Jennifer Harrington, interview, November 14, 1990.

27. Terry Green, interviews.

28. Liljegren, interview.

29. L. Steve Carpenter (park manager, Jordanelle State Park), personal communication to Daniel McCool, April 5, 1994 (in possession of editor).

30. Rainer Jaaksen, "Recreational and Spatial Boating Patterns: Theory and Management," *Leisure Sciences* 11 (1) (1989): 85–98.

31. "Jordanelle Job May Create Recreational Problems," *Salt Lake Tribune,* August 27, 1989.

32. L. Steven Carpenter, personal communication.

33. L. Steven Carpenter (park manager, Jordanelle State Park), "End-of-Year Status Report" (December 1993).

34. Blank, *Community Tourism Imperative,* pp. 99–105, 175–81.

35. This is not an uncommon practice. See Grant McConnell, *Private Power and American Democracy* (New York: Vintage Books, 1966); Thodore Lowi, *The End of Liberalism,* 2d ed. (New York: W. W. Norton, 1979); Paul Culhane, *Public Lands Politics* (Baltimore: Johns Hopkins Press, 1981); Randal Ripley and Grace Franklin, *Congress, the Bureaucracy, and Public Policy,* 5th ed. (Pacific Grove, CA: Brooks/Cole, 1991), chapter four; Frank Baumgartner and Bryan Jones, *Agendas and Instability in American Politics* (Chicago: University of Chicago Press, 1993).

36. Title 63-11-17.1, UCA, as amended.

37. Terry Green (planning manager, UPDR), personal communication to Daniel McCool, March 4, 1994 (in possession of editor).

38. Liljegren, interview.

39. Maw, interview.

40. J. G. Mitchell, "Uncluttering Yosemite," *Audubon* 11 (1990): 72–94. The Yosemite concession was recently sold.

41. Alston Chase, *Playing God in Yellowstone* (San Diego: Harvest HBJ, 1987).

42. Blank, *Community Tourism Imperative,* pp. 99–105, 175–81.

PART III

Alternative Uses and Sources

In his annual report for 1991/92, Leroy Hooton, director of the Salt Lake City Department of Public Utilities, identified a litany of vexing issues facing water policymakers: "Antiquated water laws, conservation and its relationship to revenue needs, and environmental impacts to fish habitat [have] surfaced as major issues."[1] In the face of such daunting challenges, policymakers have been searching for new concepts of water sources and water uses. In the following three chapters we see evidence of a developing relationship between new political and legal aspects of water policy, as well as technical advances.

For most cities the preeminent question regarding water is supply; how can they obtain additional sources of clean water as the city grows? One method of solving this problem is to build new dams and reservoirs. Another option is to buy water from farmers that can make more money selling water than using it; this is the "water ranching" strategy discussed in the first chapter. A third alternative is conservation, which simply means that water suppliers, and individual users, find ways to use water more efficiently. The water that is saved as a result of this conservation then becomes a new "source" of water.

For most of its history, Salt Lake City has relied on exchanges and structural solutions to augment its water supply. But in 1993, after seven years of drought, the city began to consider conservation as an option. In addition, the 1992 CUP Completion Act mandates a specific level of water conservation. While this is a new area for Salt Lake City, there is a lot we can learn from other western cities that began water conservation programs years ago. Ann Pole's chapter explains the various strategies that several western cities have implemented to increase water-use efficiency. Critics of conservation as a "supply" often claim that the amount of water saved is not significant, but the programs utilized by other cities make it quite clear that conservation can yield very significant water savings, and at a low cost compared to structural solutions. The potential water savings for Utah cities may be even more dramatic; according to a recent study, Utah has the highest per capita water consumption rate of any state in the nation.[2]

The effectiveness of conservation can be illustrated by a few examples. Recent studies conducted by Professor Frank Williams at Brigham Young University indicate that Utahns may use twice the amount of water their lawns actually need.[3] The city of West Jordan recently installed a computerized system that helps the city avoid overwatering; it will save an estimated 25 million gallons of water each year.[4] Substantial savings would also result from switching to grasses that require less water, such as grama and fescue. It is conceivable that simply by avoiding lawn overwatering and switching to low-water grasses, Salt Lake City could save more water than will be delivered to the city by the CUP (20,000 acre-feet). The question is which is cheaper: planting grama grass and watering lawns efficiently, or paying for a big government water project?

Another example of conservation is water reuse, which makes water available for secondary uses, meaning outdoor applications, not drinking water. The Central Valley Water Reclamation Facility is currently developing a project to reuse 27,600 acre-feet of water. This project, partially funded through the CUP Completion Act's conservation program, is on the cutting edge of innovative solutions to water supply problems.[5] The Salt Lake Valley's two other water treatment facilities—South Valley and Salt Lake City—could also develop such a program, which would make available another 30,000 acre-feet of water for secondary use.

The potential water savings from these reuse projects would be greatly enhanced if all new housing developments were required to install dual water systems.[6] Several Utah municipalities already use dual watering systems, which means that potable water is delivered only for indoor usage, and irrigation-quality water, which is more plentiful and cheaper, is used for lawns and gardens.[7]

Critics of conservation often claim that we will have to change our "lifestyle" if we adopt conservation measures. But unless you are an ungulate or live in your yard, switching grasses, watering efficiently, using low-water appliances, and recycling water would hardly constitute a "lifestyle" change. Critics also charge that conservation will make Salt Lake City "brown and treeless." However, trees and shrubs actually conserve water and are part of the conservation strategy for reducing usage.[8]

Water development agencies in the Salt Lake Valley have spent years attempting to develop reliable supplies of surface water, but beneath our feet is another source of water—ground-water—that may be less visible but no less important. Currently Salt Lake City derives only 12.9 percent of its water from wells. According to hydrological studies, it would be possible to pump an additional 241,000 acre-feet of groundwater in the Salt Lake Basin without lowering the water table (compare that figure with the 70,000 acre-feet the CUP will deliver to the city and county).[9] And pumping groundwater is one of the cheapest means of obtaining water. At the same time that there is a growing public demand for clean groundwater, we are just beginning to develop the technical capabilities to detect and cleanse groundwater pollutants.[10] Much of the discussion in Shawn Twitchell's chapter concerns efforts to make changes in policy that can keep up with technological advances and our increasing understanding of groundwater quality and hydrology.

The same can be said of the chapter on instream flow by Ann Wechsler; only recently have scientists developed the capability to quantify instream flow requirements for fish, wildlife, and habitat. But developments in the law of instream flow are much more than technical questions; a growing emphasis on instream flow uses reflects a dramatic change in how society wants to use scarce water supplies.

All three of these authors are writing about relatively new developments in water policy that are driven by changing values and technical advances. Traditionally, water policy focused narrowly on diverting surface water for consumption; these chapters indicate that our concept of water management has expanded far beyond that. Clearly the various elements of water policy—surface diversions, groundwater, water quality, changing uses—cannot be isolated from each other; hydrologically and politically they are integral parts of a larger system. The authors demonstrate that while new attitudes and approaches often encounter hostility, significant change still occurs.

Notes

1. Salt Lake City Department of Public Utilities, "Annual Report, 1991/92, (Salt Lake City, 1992), p. 2. The report offered some good news, however: the city's culinary water usage remained nearly constant for five years, which contradicts the predictions made by planners of continual growth in demand.

2. U.S. Geological Survey, "Estimated Use of Water in the United States in 1990," circular no. 1081 (Washington, D.C., 1993).

3. Frank Williams (professor of horticulture at Brigham Young University), telephone interview, March 15, 1995.

4. Utah Division of Water Resources, *Utah Water Education and Conservation Newsletter* (Oct. 1994): 1.

5. Central Utah Water Conservancy District, "Scoping Information Summary, for the Central Valley Water Reuse Project" (Orem, Utah, January 1995).

6. South Jordan and West Jordan require developers to install secondary water systems, and Kearns is considering such a requirement. Water reuse programs could supply large quantities of cheap water to these secondary systems.

7. Towns and municipalities that have installed dual water systems for all or part of their outdoor water usage include Parowan, Gunnison, Spring City, Payson, Kaysville, Beaver, Hyrum, Farr West, Plain City, Draper, Lindon, South Jordan, West Jordan, and Lehi. It is quite expensive to retrofit existing water systems with dual pipes, but requiring dual systems for all new development is usually economical, especially if water is priced at its true market value.

8. F. Herbert Borman, Diana Balmori, and Gordon Geballe, *Redesigning the American Lawn* (New Haven, Conn.: Yale University Press, 1993).

9. A. G. Hely, R. W. Mower, and C. A. Harr, "Summary of Water Resources of Salt Lake County, Utah," Technical Publication no. 34, Utah Department of Natural Resources (Salt Lake City, 1971); Jay M. Bagley, "Problems of Providing Least-Cost Increments of Water Supply in Urbanizing Situations," paper presented at the ASCE International Conference on Resource Mobilization for Drinking Water Supply, San Juan, Puerto Rico, May 26–29, 1987.

10. For example, the U.S. Geological Survey will soon begin the largest water quality assessment ever conducted on the Wasatch Front. This $6 million study will use the latest technology to detect organic contaminants, heavy metals, and other forms of water-borne pollutants; *Salt Lake Tribune*, April 18, 1993.

CHAPTER FIVE

Municipal Water Conservation

Ann Pole

Developing reservoirs as storage facilities for the seasonal fluctuations of rivers and streams has historically been synonymous with water conservation in the western United States. These facilities, combined with water diversion and delivery systems, provide the present water supply to rural and urban communities of the West. As the current systems are tapped to their maximum capacities and remaining water supplies become allocated for municipal, agricultural, industrial, recreational, and instream flow uses, the unallocated supply available to sustain community growth diminishes.

While water suppliers can choose to seek new water sources, either through new water developments (storage and delivery systems) or reallocation of current supplies to more valued uses (such as from agricultural to municipal use), these alternatives are becoming increasingly costly, politically and/or environmentally unpopular, or simply impractical. On the other hand, increasing the efficiency of consumer use of current supplies may generate predictable, permanent reductions in water demands and change the nature of long-term supply planning. Yet can water managers realistically look to demand-reducing methods as a new source of supply?

"Water conservation is doing with one gallon what any fool could do with ten."[1] Conservation in this sense involves both behavioral changes by the communities affected and actual physical (technological) changes in delivery systems and plumbing devices. When water suppliers consider conservation alternatives, they must appraise both their demand situation and the numerous methods available to the consumer. Suppliers must assess public willingness to comply and the degree to which individuals will change their lifestyles. Suppliers must also look to the operations of their own system for more efficient methods of supplying water to the consumer. In short, managers must identify wasteful practices within their own systems and within the communities they supply; only then can municipalities work to reduce their demands.

In Utah as in other states, conservation advocates suggest this method as an alternative to large-scale, taxpayer subsidized storage and delivery projects such as the Central Utah Project. Advocating a combination of conservation and growth-limiting policies may be necessary in the future, but conservation methods alone can provide consumption savings even without the politically difficult goal of growth limitation. However, as water managers suggest, relying solely on demand reduction to create new water supplies may be a dangerous path during years of drought.

This chapter describes the various conservation methods available to municipalities and analyzes the viability of water conservation in terms of demand reduction as a means to create new water supplies and sustain community growth. Conservation programs of selected municipalities from Arizona, California, and Nevada were studied in terms of program extensiveness, effectiveness, and resulting "new" supply generated. These areas have initiated conservation for different reasons, and the extensiveness of each area's program reflects the reliability of available water sources. Comparing the results of these programs provides information that may assist the efforts of Salt Lake City and Utah to plan for future water supplies. This information can also help to develop a broader public awareness program, increase the effectiveness of voluntary measures, and aid in the implementation of new codes and ordinances, if and when water managers perceive the need for increased conservation.

Motivation and Success

When exploring techniques for encouraging conservation, planners must identify the target and severity of need for
conservation. In the mid 1970s, Tucson, Arizona, initiated the
"Beat the Peak" program to curb the peak flows that were ham-
pering the city's ability to supply water. By the early 1980s, both
Tucson and Phoenix, Arizona, were planning for long-term conservation measures to help replenish groundwater aquifers, in
keeping with newly passed Arizona groundwater legislation. In
1986 WestPac, the privately run water supplier for Reno,
Nevada, encouraged a peak reduction campaign to delay construction of new treatment facilities. The conservation program
initiated in Las Vegas, Nevada, intends to apply long-term measures to reduce the demand for costly water importation.

Some municipalities in California have water supplies that
barely meet population demands during years of below average
precipitation. Currently, these communities use restrictions and
rationing, in addition to voluntary measures to stem demand.
During the worst years of the most recent drought, cities such as
Santa Barbara had "water cops" to patrol neighborhoods and
ticket water wasters.

Salt Lake City and its surrounding communities have supplies in large storage facilities to support current demands and
will have new supplies to support predicted growth through
2010.[2] After seven years of below average precipitation in the
late 1980s, the city still had not promoted restrictions in use or
developed widespread public awareness campaigns to reduce
consumption, even though such measures could extend the
area's water supply for decades to come. For Utah's water managers, this situation demonstrates the success of past planning:
no one needed to curtail any activities as a result of the drought.

Nevertheless, Utah should look to those places that have
taken the lead in conserving water. Table 5.1 shows the extent
of conservation activities of various western municipalities.

Table 5.1

Conservation Programs in Selected Municipalities

Municipality	Public Awareness Program	Voluntary Measures	Mandatory Measures	Age of Program	Full-time Conservation Staff
Phoenix	Yes	Retrofit program Reduced watering	Plumbing code change	ten years	thirteen
Tucson	Yes	Retrofit Program Reduced watering	Plumbing code change Recycled water in decorative fountains	thirteen years	eleven
Las Vegas	Yes		None	nine months	five
Reno	Yes	Reduced watering	Meters in new construction	four years	none
Santa Barbara	Yes	Retrofit plumbing	No outdoor watering until end of drought	"Always"	twelve
Marin County	Yes	Rationing	Plumbing code change Turf size limited	four dry years	twelve
Salt Lake City	Yes		None	ten years	none

Compiled from interviews with water officials in selected communities

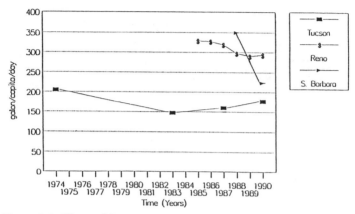

Figure 5.1. Effects of Conservation Programs on Consumption

Figure 5.1 shows differences in per capita consumption before and after the initiation of a program for Tucson, Reno, and Santa Barbara. The data demonstrate that each community experienced a decline in per capita consumption. The largest decline over the shortest period of time occurred, not surprisingly, in Santa Barbara, where consumption dropped 42 percent in five years, while reservoir levels fell; Reno, with the least comprehensive conservation program of the three, showed a 13 percent decline between 1986 and 1990. These results show that even a small-scale awareness program can change consumers' habits; in times of drought, the crisis situation can produce large-scale declines in water use.

Most water suppliers use annual per capita consumption numbers to demonstrate consumption changes, although the unit does not necessarily reflect changes due to the conservation program itself. Suppliers derive the number by dividing the total gallons of water sent out per day by the number of people served and multiplying by the number of days per year. Several factors influence per capita consumption: precipitation and temperature variations; population base and associated commercial, industrial, and agricultural uses; and average per capita income of the water users. Jeffrey DeWitt of the city of Phoenix cited a study completed by his department that showed a fluctuation of seven gallons per capita per day, for every $1°F$

temperature change over the same day of the previous year.[3] However, over a long-term period, per capita use within a community should reflect a change due to conservation measures.

Demand Reduction Methods

Conservation programs can reduce water consumption at two points: in the supply and delivery system and at the point of consumption. Water use by the consumer can be further subdivided into industrial-commercial use and residential use. The following sections discuss programs directed toward the residential user and describe water supply and delivery alternatives considered by the water supplier. Many water managers are concerned that conservation methods might require lifestyle changes that the public might be unwilling to undergo; while this may be true for some methods, water planners can identify and employ the least controversial methods and inform the public of options that require different degrees of change.

Residential Conservation Practices—Outdoor Use

Residential conservation programs generally focus on the two categories of indoor and outdoor use. In some regions of the West, outdoor use (lawn watering and outdoor swimming pools) constitutes between 35 percent and 75 percent of total residential consumption, with the majority of use occurring during the summer months. Indoor use remains fairly constant throughout the year, with the main use occurring in the bathroom.[4] Other indoor activities include dishwashing, laundry, kitchen and bathroom sinks, and general utility (see Fig 5.2). Overall, the average household of four consumes from 1/3 to 1 acre-foot (325,872 gallons) of water each year. Conservation programs target these residential uses with long-term measures to lower annual per capita consumption.

Since outdoor use comprises such a large proportion of residential demand and is perceived as relatively unnecessary, particularly during droughts, this type of consumption can readily be curbed. The major suggestion is to change lawn maintenance routines. Recommended strategies call for watering only as

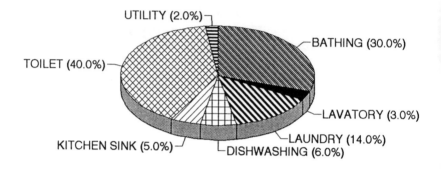

Figure 5.2. Water Usage by Fixture as a Percentage of Total Indoor Use (from "Wasatch Front Total Water Management Study," 1988).

needed (overwatering turf is a large source of water waste) and watering during cooler times of the day to limit evaporation losses. Monthly reminders arriving with the water bill also can discuss other simple tips for efficient water use. The emphasis of these suggestions is simplicity; most agencies seek to make practical and permanent changes in day-to-day water use.

A new and increasingly popular water-saving strategy for outdoor use is Xeriscape—landscaping with drought resistant or desert vegetation. In many areas of the western United States, native plants provide garden beauty with lower water requirements and low maintenance once established (usually after one or two years). Alternative grasses have been developed that require less water than the favored Kentucky bluegrass species. How much less is an issue that is still debated, indicating that more research needs to be completed before new turf types are promoted. Factors such as transpiration ratios and soil types affect how much water is needed, and water needs even for Kentucky bluegrass can vary widely. Many believe that bluegrass is overwatered in most cases.[5]

Xeriscape emphasizes landscape design in addition to providing vegetation alternatives. Tucson residents are changing to Xeriscape while allowing small areas to remain as turf. Phoenix, Las Vegas, and the state of Utah provide residents with either economic incentives or information (or both) to encourage this alternative. Las Vegas went to the state legislature to get permission to allow desert landscaping in residential areas.[6] John Wohlmuth, senior administrative assistant in Palm Desert, California, reports that Xeriscape on public properties (around buildings, roadways) costs $0.04 per square foot to maintain, whereas water-loving grasses and palms reminiscent of desert oases cost $0.16 per square foot to maintain.[7] The city of Phoenix estimates that limiting turf size and using Xeriscape will result in water savings of 2,600 acre-feet per year by 1995 and 19,100 acre-feet by 2040.[8] The Utah Department of Transportation has begun experiments applying Xeriscape techniques to areas along the Salt Lake Valley I-215 freeway and interchanges. This program is new, and results will not be available for several years. Though water savings on an individual basis may appear quite small, changing a community's collective outdoor water use provides significant water savings.

Indoor Use

Inside the home, water suppliers recognize many behavioral and mechanical changes consumers can make to save water. These are relatively simple techniques requiring little or no capital investment, yet they save significant amounts of water. The simplest suggestions include eliminating wasteful habits.

Taking this a step further, fixing leaks and changing plumbing
fixtures are inexpensive yet impressively effective water-saving
techniques. A slow, steady drip from a leaky faucet (100 drops
per minute) will waste 350 gallons per month.[9] Displacement
devices in toilet tanks can reduce consumption from 5–6 gallons
per flush to 3.5 gallons per flush at a cost of less than ten dollars
for installation. Inserting faucet and shower aerators reduces
flows, and therefore consumption, for fifty cents per installation.
An aerator can reduce a sink faucet flow from up to 12 gallons
per minute to under 4 gallons; likewise, a shower aerator can
reduce flows from up to 8 gallons per minute to 2.3 gallons. An
average family using each of these devices could save approximately 30 gallons per day.[10] These minor and inexpensive
changes are equated with permanently reduced consumption
and the creation of "new" supply; they are therefore popular
suggestions made by water conservation advocates.

In Tucson the "Casa del Agua" was developed as a model
home for the promotion of indoor and outdoor conservation
practices. The home uses water-saving indoor plumbing fixtures, collects rainwater for outdoor use, and recycles "gray
water" (household wastewater excluding toilet and kitchen
waste) for outdoor irrigation and indoor toilet use. These latter
two technologies involve considerably more planning, expense,
and in the case of gray-water use, health considerations. Even
so, this three-bedroom, two-bathroom home with three residents consumed half the water of the average Tucson family in
its first eighteen months of operation (161,844 gallons versus
347,080 gallons for the average family). Tucson Water and the
Pima County Wastewater Management Department sponsor the
home, and the program generates valuable data for individuals
and communities facing diminishing water supplies. For
Tucson water managers, the project "is paving the way for a
more water-efficient Tucson lifestyle, a lifestyle that requires
only minimal changes to reap noticeable benefits."[11]

Conservation in the Supply and Delivery System

Municipal suppliers must also examine their own supply
and delivery systems to identify conservation techniques that

can eliminate waste and reduce water demand. There are many such methods, including leak detection in delivery pipes, metering of consumers, the development of reuse systems, and pricing. Traditionally, when a supplier anticipated a shortage, it developed a new supply in the form of a reservoir. Now with the larger water sources already developed, suppliers themselves are turning to more efficient practices.

"Investing in leak detection and repair is one of the most universally cost-effective conservation measures urban suppliers can undertake."[12] Water lost in the delivery of treated supplies is referred to as "unaccounted for water." WestPac, the private water utility in Reno, reports a 10 percent loss due to leaks and meter error.[13] The city of Phoenix reported a loss of 13 percent in its system in 1988. The city's goal is to reduce this factor to 9 percent of its production; while the detection equipment and program are expected to cost $40,000 initially, savings are estimated at 13,500 acre-feet per year by the year 2000 and 20,700 acre-feet per year by 2040.[14] Salt Lake City Public Utilities estimates that it loses 3–7 percent of water produced and admits that it often does not have the money to repair leaks.[15]

Water reuse consists of treating wastewater generated by a municipality back to drinking water standards or to standards for yard or irrigation uses. Several factors impede the development of water reuse: treatment costs, pumping costs, the availability of dual water systems, and health concerns. However, if these problems are solved, the water savings can be substantial. The Central Valley Water Reclamation Facility project discussed in the introduction to this part of the book is one example of water reuse.[16]

Water reuse should be viewed as an option for industry as well. Industries should be encouraged to purchase municipal wastewater at a reduced rate or to recycle their own wastewater by using it in other plant processes. Utah industry reuses 784,000 acre-feet of municipal water per year and recycles more water than any other class of water user—432 million acre-feet per year.[17]

Metering and Pricing

"Metering users is the best conservation practice; all of Salt Lake City is metered."[18] Apparently the best method of all, making water users accountable for their level of use, should be encouraged by water providers. Figure 5.3 compares communities' average per capita consumption with their use of meters. Note that Las Vegas and Reno supply water to numerous hotels and managers from these areas assert they have no control over this level of use. Likewise, Salt Lake City experiences a large daytime population increase due to commercial and industrial activities; higher per capita consumption rates result from these influences. Metering community water users does not guarantee frugal water use, so water managers need to combine the use of water meters with other conservation strategies, such as pricing or setting optimal water-use goals, in order to gain the most value from meter installations.

The issue of pricing represents the major political aspect of water conservation. Critics of below-cost pricing bemoan the fact that in such dry regions as the western United States, water rates are low and consumption is high: "Urban residents in the West generally pay less than half the price paid for water in the East which helps explain why publicly supplied withdrawals are 45 percent higher per capita in the West."[19] In Salt Lake City water is a real bargain; the average price is $15 per 3,000 gallons, compared to a national average of $33. In Tucson, Arizona, the same amount of water costs $45.[20] Making water too cheap "produces a host of market distortions and leads to inefficiencies and 'overconsumption'."[21] This occurs primarily in regions where large storage and delivery systems were developed with the use of local, state, and especially federal subsidies.

Nonetheless, who will promote change in current pricing policies? Three council members in Tucson were recalled between 1976 and 1977 because they increased water rates and pumping charges in response to record water consumption.[22] While water consumption is generally recognized as being tied to pricing (that is, if water prices increase, consumption will decrease), price increases would need to be substantial, and unpopular, for significant decreases in consumption to occur.[23]

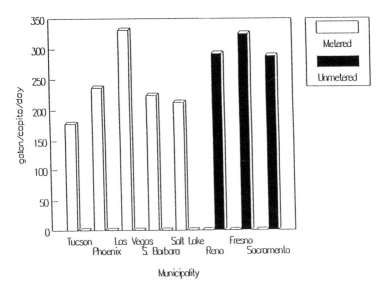

Figure 5.3. Water Consumption and Meter Use.

Phoenix residents, responding to a survey administered by the water department, indicated that raising prices was an unacceptable means of encouraging conservation.[24] The Central Utah Water Conservancy District received a similar response in a survey conducted in 1993.[25]

In Utah a 1985 opinion poll clearly demonstrated that residents preferred the construction of additional supply facilities over increased water rates (with subsequent decline in water consumption) as the method to increase future supplies.[26] Of course this may be because the costs of creating new supplies can be hidden through various taxing schemes (see chapter one), while direct price increases are obvious to the ratepayer. Since 1985, however, the state has experienced a nearly continuous drought. For the first time in its history, the Salt Lake City Water Department emphasized water conservation in early 1993, by proposing an increasing block-rate pricing structure.[27] The plan was voted down by the city council and the mayor, because all water users' rates would increase initially, and that was politically unpopular. However, in April of 1995 the city council approved a 6 percent rate hike for the summer months, when water usage peaks.

By October 1995 the Central Utah Water Conservancy District will complete a water pricing study under the requirements of the CUP Completion Act. This study will examine the impact of different pricing strategies on water use and revenue changes. The District can then decide to implement a pricing strategy to assist its conservation goals, as set forth by the Completion Act.[28] While this change would affect only CUP water purchasers, the information may influence a broader rate restructuring by municipalities throughout the state.

Utah: Attitudes and Strategies for Conservation

With the passage of the CUP Completion Act, Utahns may finally be encouraged to make better use of their water resources. This will certainly be true for agricultural and municipal purchasers of project water. The act requires that the Central Utah Water Conservancy District conserve a minimum of 30,000 acre-feet of water per year by 2010. In addition, a nine-member Utah Water Conservation Advisory Board was established in 1994; its task is to write a report on proposed standards and regulations for water conservation in the service areas purchasing CUP water.[29] Dan Beard, the director of the U.S. Bureau of Reclamation, recently predicted that the "water conservation requirements of the Central Utah Water Project Completion Act will make Utah a leader in innovative approaches."[30] Commissioner Beard has made water conservation the Bureau's "highest priority."[31]

The District's "innovative approaches" will be more extensive than those of the past fifteen years. The latter consisted primarily of educational materials for kindergarten through sixth grade students and the introduction of Xeriscape information for landscape architects and other interested individuals. Local and state water managers were reluctant to introduce legislation requiring plumbing code and use restrictions because of the political implications and the loss of revenue to suppliers resulting from demand reduction. Now, however, the District and its customers are federally mandated to conserve water.

This mandate stems from the fact that Utah water suppliers do not actively conserve water, yet they continue to plan and seek federal funding for large-scale water projects. Many Utah communities are in a peculiar position among the municipalities studied; after seven years of below average rainfall (from 1987), no widespread water conservation campaigns have been initiated. Water managers did express concern that water storage facilities were slipping to new lows, however. An eighth dry year may dramatically curtail Utah's extravagant water use. And yet the state's municipalities were far better off than Santa Barbara, which suffered the loss of its green landscapes during the same years.

Water managers locally and statewide point to the network of large water storage facilities as the reason why Utah citizens can continue their consumption patterns uninterrupted by a prolonged drought. They claim that this is their role in water management: capture the water and make it available all year, to smooth out an otherwise erratic supply. Utah planned for population growth and thus has water supplies available for a water-extravagant community.

In addition, water managers point out that there are risks in a water supply created through conservation methods. Residents in Santa Barbara and Marin County, California, during the 1970s proposed to limit population by voting down measures to fund additional water supply delivery projects. Four years of below average rainfall then made these communities dependent on lifestyle-changing conservation methods and temporary outside water supplies.

In Santa Barbara a population "cap" determined in the early 1980s, was just being reached by middecade, while supplies rapidly dropped over the same four years.[32] The city then spent $38 million on a desalination plant, which was completed just prior to the end of their drought. Built as an emergency facility, the plant will be upgraded to a permanent facility, but currently it is not supplying water to the community.

Water managers in Utah argue that relying on conservation as a new source of supply does not give a "safety margin" during times of drought and puts the population as a whole at risk for lifestyle-changing measures during a time of severe and extended drought, although no studies confirm this assertion. However, a study by the Utah Water Research Laboratory concluded that "security against shortfall is purchased at a very high price" and further indicated that "the acceptable risk of shortfall as arbitrarily selected by public officials (e.g. 5 percent), may not reflect society's preferences for risk."[33] Perhaps water managers in Utah misjudge the public's preferences, and more opportunity may exist for active demand reduction than previously believed.

Water managers also contend that there is little incentive for the consumer to conserve, since water is available and cheap. Conservation practices would therefore decrease the amount of water sold by utilities, and water rates would subsequently increase with the consumer and supplier being no better off economically. Barry Saunders noted that "water agencies rely on water sales and do not have an interest in curbing water use."[34] During the 1977–78 drought, Salt Lake City Public Utilities experienced a 30 percent loss in income directly related to voluntary conservation measures practiced by the public.[35] While basing sewer rates on winter use (essentially indoor use) has led to a 10 percent decline in water use by customers, a substantial decrease in water use during the unusually rainy spring season of 1991 prompted discussion of a possible rate increase to cover revenue losses once again. Though no rate increase occurred, Salt Lake City's pricing strategy reflects that of a community with an abundant, reliable source of water. Indeed, price can persuade customers to use less, but in Salt Lake City the objective has always been to encourage customers to use more.

Conclusion

The Clark County, Nevada, *Conservation Action Plan* argues that "conservation is our cheapest source of new water."[36] However, other planners take a different view: "Additional storage facilities in areas that experience recurring annual water shortages are the best source of additional supplies."[37] Ultimately, the choice between new storage or conservation may depend on economics: new reservoirs bring more security, but can communities afford them?

The water savings from conservation can be quite significant. Phoenix estimates it will be conserving about 50,000 acre-feet of water per year by the year 2040, with the full implementation of long-term measures,[38] and concludes, "our water resources can be managed to sustain projected growth."[39] There are certainly opposing viewpoints concerning the role of water conservation in providing new public supply. Although municipal suppliers in Utah express reluctance toward creating reliable new supplies through demand reduction practices, no comprehensive studies have been completed that compare conservation with other forms of supply in terms of relative costs and benefits, environmental impact, and certainty of supply.

The data presented here indicate that increased water awareness and voluntary restrictions on water use can decrease residential use by 10 percent. Depending on the current vigilance of suppliers to operate their supply and delivery systems more efficiently, this decrease in overall demand could be substantially higher.

The key to water use and demand management, as with other resources, should be efficiency. Technological and behavioral changes have led to significant reductions in home heating fuel and gasoline consumption.[40] At some point, this will also be true for water; before investing in new supply and delivery systems, communities will choose more efficient technologies and behaviors.

This trend has begun in cities in the West as well as across the country, but the United States lags behind its counterparts in other regions of the world. Per capita water use in Salt Lake City is about 220 gallons per day (for the country as a whole, the average is about 110 gallons per day); for West Germany and France, the figure is about 40 gallons per day and for Israel about 35 gallons per day.[41] Clearly, greater efficiency can be achieved for the Salt Lake City area; the cost in terms of lifestyle and technology remains unaddressed.

Water managers and the community must be realistic about the potential value of conservation when considering expensive, large-scale developments. For a consumer (who will also become the source of funding for new projects), conservation provides an inexpensive alternative to increased supply. For water managers, it will be a challenge to convince the public that conservation is a form of water "supply." Many people still think that conservation means artificial reservoirs. However, every dollar spent on water storage is one dollar less for research and technological improvements for conservation methods. Though it is renewable, water is a finite resource capable of supporting only a limited number of individuals; that number depends on how efficiently they use their water.

Notes

1. L. M. Eisel, "Water Conservation: The Federal Viewpoint," in *Proceedings on the Conference on Water Conservation: Needs and Implementing Strategies* (New York: American Society of Engineers, 1979), p. 22.

2. David Ovard (Salt Lake County Water Conservancy District), interview, November 29, 1989.

3. Jeffrey DeWitt (water resources analyst, City of Phoenix Water and Wastewater Department), telephone interview, December 3, 1990.

4. U.S. Bureau of Reclamation and Utah Division of Water Resources, "Wasatch Front Total Water Management Study—Jordan River Basin," draft version (Salt Lake City, 1988), figure VI-9.

5. Ira Bickford (Utah Department of Transportation), telephone interview, April 4, 1994. According to an information packet provided by the National Xeriscape Council, in a twenty-week growing season, Kentucky bluegrass requires 18 gallons of water per square foot, fescue requires 10 gallons, and blue grama grass requires 0–3 gallons. However, these figures are widely disputed.

6. Clark County Public Works Department, *Clark County Water Resource Strategy: Conservation Action Plan* (Las Vegas, Nev., 1990).

7. Burt Nydes, "Climates for Change: Legacy of the Drought," *American City and County* 104 (June 1989): 40.

8. City of Phoenix Water and Wastewater Department, Water Conservation and Resources Division, *Phoenix Water Resources Plan* (Phoenix, Ariz., 1990), p. 85.

9. Tucson Water, "Casa del Agua Information Paper" (Tucson, Ariz., undated), p. 2.

10. T. C. Hughes et al., *Economic Evaluation of Conservation Concepts for Municipal Water Systems* (Logan, Utah: Utah Water Research Laboratory, Utah State University, 1986), p. 98.

11. Tucson Water, "Casa del Agua Information Paper," p. 1.

12. Sandra Postel, *Water Conservation: The Untapped Alternative* (Washington, D.C.: Worldwatch Institute, 1985), p. 45.

13. Rick Mozier (Western Pacific Utility), telephone interview, November 12, 1990.

14. City of Phoenix, *Phoenix Water Resources Plan*, pp. 88–89.

15. Wendall Evanson (Salt Lake City Public Utilities), interview, November 19, 1990.

16. Successful water reuse projects have been developed in Arizona, Colorado, Wyoming, and especially California.

17. U.S. Bureau of Reclamation and Utah Division of Water Resources, *Wasatch Front Total Water Management*, p. 90.

18. Evanson, interview.

19. Kenneth D. Frederick, "Overview," in *Scarce Water and Institutional Change*, ed. by Kenneth D. Frederick (Washington, D.C.: Resources for the Future, Inc., 1986), p. 6.

20. *Deseret News*, June 23, 1993, p. B-1.

21. Richard A. Berk et al., *Water Shortage: Lessons in Conservation from the Great California Drought, 1976–1977* (Cambridge, Mass.: Abt Books, 1981), p. 6.

22. Tucson Water, *Make Every Drop Count* (Tucson, 1988), p. 4.

23. There is considerable evidence that water is "price-elastic," meaning that a marginal increase in price will result in a significant reduction in demand. See B. C. Conley, "Price Elasticity of Demand for Water in Southern California," *Annals of Regional Science* 1 (December 1967): 180–89; Steven Hanke, "A Method for Integrating Engineering and Economic Planning," *Journal of the American Water Works Association* 70 (August 1978): 487091; Peter Rogers, "Water: Not as Cheap as You'd Think," *Technology Review* 89 (8) (1986): 32.

24. City of Phoenix, *Phoenix Water Resources Plan*, p. 80.

25. Central Utah Water Conservancy District, "Water Management Improvement Studies Survey" (Orem, Utah, August 1993).

26. U.S. Bureau of Reclamation and Utah Division of Water Resources, *Wasatch Front Total Water Management*, p. 157.

27. *Deseret News*, January 29, 1993, p. B-1.

28. Public Law 207-575, sec. 207 (102d Congress), October 30, 1992.

29. Utah Division of Water Resources, "Utah Water Education and Conservation Newsletter" (April 1994).

30. Quoted in the *Salt Lake Tribune*, November 8, 1993.

31. Upper Colorado River Region, *Water Conservation Notes* (December 1994):1.

32. Lisa Weeks (water conservation officer, Santa Barbara Public Utilities), interview, December 3, 1990.

33. Hughes et al., *Economic Evaluation of Conservation Concepts*, p. 121.

34. Barry Saunders (associate director, Utah Division of Water Resources), interview, November 12, 1990.

35. Evanson, interview.

36. Clark County Public Works Department, *Conservation Action Plan*, p. 10.

37. U.S. Bureau of Reclamation and Utah Division of Water Resources, *Wasatch Front Total Water Management*, p. 5–2.

38. City of Phoenix, *Phoenix Water Resources Plan*, pp. 83–89. In comparison, note that Salt Lake City has contracted for 20,000 acre-feet of water from the CUP; would it be cheaper to conserve that amount?

39. City of Phoenix Water and Wastewater Department, Water Conservation and Resources Division, "Highlights of the City of Phoenix Water Conservation Program," draft version (Phoenix, 1990), p. 8.

40. See William Ophuls and Stephen Boyan, Jr., *Ecology and the Politics of Scarcity Revisited* (New York: W. H. Freeman, 1992), pp. 104–9; David Howard Davis, *Energy Politics*, 3d ed. (New York: St. Martin's Press, 1982), pp. 260–64; Robert Stobaugh and Daniel Yergin, eds., *Energy Future*, 3d ed. (New York: Random House, 1983), chap. 6.

41. Postel, *Water Conservation*, p. 40.

CHAPTER SIX

The Evolution of Groundwater Policy

Shawn Twitchell

In Utah water is a rigorously protected possession; water quantity has been the area of greatest concern and regulation. Although legal recognition of groundwater as a usable resource has lagged somewhat behind surface water regulation, groundwater has become a major resource for the citizens of the state. Historically, most policymakers have considered groundwater use a private activity that should not be regulated.

But in recent years there has been considerable political activity concerning both the quality and quantity of groundwater. Changing values and technological advancements have served as the catalysts for change in this policy area.[1] This chapter reviews the political and legal aspects of groundwater in the state and examines some future issues.

Quantity

In Utah the subject of groundwater quantity is related to groundwater stocks and the legal doctrine of prior appropriation, which determines who is entitled to the available stocks and for what purpose. Before discussing appropriation, a brief review of the actual supply of groundwater in the state will place the legal issues in perspective.

A review of the increasing consumption of groundwater in the state and the changing nature of its use reveal the basis for potential conflicts in the appropriation of groundwater. Table 6.1 identifies selected groundwater units and shows the percentage of change in aquifer withdrawal rates over a minimum time period of at least ten years ending in 1979.

Table 6.1
Change in Utah Groundwater Withdrawals to 1979

Groundwater Unit	Years Reviewed	Percent Change
Grouse Creek Valley	1967–1979	+50
Park Valley	1968–1979	+520
Curlew Valley	1969–1979	+23
Cache Valley	1967–1979	-2.0
East Shore	1969–1979	+64
Salt Lake Valley	1968–1979	+27
Cedar Valley	1965–1979	+259
Northern Utah Valley	1963–1979	+47
Southern Utah Valley	1966–1979	-22
Sevier Desert	1964–1979	+50
Snake Valley	1964–1979	+224
Pahvant Valley	1959–1979	+43
Central Virgin River Basin	1968–1979	+302

Total estimated groundwater withdrawals in 1979 = 700,480 acre-feet. Percentage changes calculated from data adapted from M. S. Bedinger, J. S. Gates, and J. R. Stark, "Maps Showing Groundwater Units and Withdrawal, Basin and Range Province, Utah" (U.S. Geological Survey, Investigations Report no. 83-4122A Washington, D.C., 1984), pp. 4–6. The source reports data from thirty-five separate authors.

Table 6.2 shows the percentage of change from 1979 to 1989 for selected groundwater units with a minimum of 15,000 acre-feet withdrawal (the major withdrawal areas in the state). From this data it is clear that overall consumption of the state's groundwater reflects an increasing population and a consequent increase in demand for groundwater. By 1990 Utahns were withdrawing 964 million gallons of groundwater each day.[2]

Between 1965 and 1979 the primary aim of groundwater withdrawals changed from agricultural use to municipal and
xxxx

Table 6.2
Change in Utah Groundwater Withdrawals
1979–1989

Groundwater Unit	Years Reviewed	Percent Change
Curlew Valley	1979–1989	+13
Cache Valley	1979–1989	-14
East Shore	1979–1989	+33
Salt Lake Valley	1979–1989	-2
Tooele Valley	1979–1989	-1
Utah and Goshen Valleys	1979–1989	+13
Pahvant Valley	1979–1989	-5
Parowan and Cedar Valleys	1979–1989	-8
Central Virgin River Valley	1979–1989	+16

Total estimated Utah groundwater withdrawals in 1989 = 851,000 acre-feet.
Percentage change 1979–1989 = +21 percent. Groundwater unit change calculated from data reported by L. R. Herbert et al. (1990), and Bedinger, Gates and Stark (1984).

industrial use along the central Wasatch Front. This area of the state includes about 77 percent of Utah's population, and has experienced the greatest increase in population during the past several decades.[3] In the densely populated Wasatch Front area (Utah and Goshen Valleys, Salt Lake Valley, and the East Shore area), withdrawals for irrigation decreased from 40 percent in 1965 to 26 percent in 1979 to less than 23 percent by 1989; groundwater withdrawn for domestic and industrial use increased from 40 percent in 1965 to 58 percent in 1979 to 61 percent in 1989.[4] An important consideration is that between 1964 and 1968, approximately 40 percent of the aquifer recharge came from irrigation seepage.[5]

Evidence of this changing use is also seen in an increased level of water rights transfers: "Since 1987, the Central Utah Water Conservancy District has held out a standing offer of $164 per acre-foot for permanent water rights. The Salt Lake County Conservancy District (a major supplier of domestic and industrial water in the Salt Lake Valley) has offered a higher price—around $250. The two entities have purchased more than

100,000 acre-feet of rights so far."[6]   It is this changing use that has significant implications for future modifications of Utah's groundwater policy.

Legal Issues in Appropriation

        Appropriation of both groundwater and surface water in Utah falls under a single set of laws and procedures. Prior to 1935, however, appropriative rights to groundwater were restricted to water serving as a source for a surface stream that encroached on another's land.[7] Ownership of groundwater that did not meet the above criteria was vested in the overlying land owner. "Under this [absolute ownership] doctrine a landowner is said to own, and has an unlimited right to withdraw, any water found beneath the owned land."[8]   In *Wrathall v. Johnson* (1935), the court expanded the appropriation doctrine to include any groundwater that could be diverted or drawn upon. Later courts upheld this position, with the exception that groundwater providing a "natural benefit" on the surface, such as vegetative growth, belongs to the overlying landowner and is not subject to appropriation. Groundwater in excess of that required to maintain the surface plants is subject to appropriation.[9]

        Current Utah statutes and case law governing appropriation of groundwater permit two legal avenues to challenge existing groundwater rights beyond the traditional theories of "first in time, first in right" and "beneficial use." The first alternative legal challenge could come from applications for appropriation of any "relic" aquifers. A relic aquifer is one which, through some geologic activity in the past, is not being recharged currently. This type of aquifer is distinct and separate from any overlying, underlying, or adjacent aquifer, and has no natural area of discharge or recharge. In Utah much of this water is in aquifers in remote West Desert regions, with the original source thought to be the ancient Lake Bonneville.[10] A legal challenge to the appropriation laws of the state could result if appropriation of these relic aquifers is attempted because of the language in the *Wrathall v. Johnson* case. Specifically at question is terminology identifying appropriable water in aquifers as continually moving from a source (presumably a recharge area) to the point of diversion. If there is no recharge source, can the water be appropriated, or would its ownership revert to the overlying landowner? This question has yet to arise in the courts. The second legal challenge concerns situations in which groundwater withdrawals have lowered a streamflow, resulting in riparian damage, but without damage to downstream appropriators. Presumably the damage would have to occur in the area where groundwater flowed into a stream, and the owner of the riparian area would be the only one with standing to challenge the groundwater withdrawals. Given the current controversy regarding maintenance and restoration of riparian zones, however, the question may be raised in the future.

Another area of possible legal action concerning groundwater appropriation is the section of the Utah Code dealing with priorities among appropriators. One possible exception is listed to the standard prior appropriation doctrine: "in times of scarcity, while priority of appropriation shall give the better right as between those using water for the same purpose, the use for domestic purposes, without unnecessary waste, shall have preference over use for all other purposes, and use for agricultural purposes shall have preference over use for any other purpose except domestic use."[11] The question is, what constitutes scarcity? To date the answer has not been provided by case law or legislation. Several entities have indicated that although water is not currently scarce, it may be in the future: "With the population of Utah a little over 1 million (1970) and projections to double by the turn of the century, it is apparent that Utah's water supply is small in relation to the State's potential water demand."[12] This estimate of a statewide population of two million in the year 2000 is still believed to be accurate.[13] Meanwhile, the question of scarcity and its relation to the larger question of "beneficial" use remains.

This is not the first review of potential conflicts that might arise from the wording of the state water code. In 1955 a committee was appointed by the Legislative Council to review state statutes and management policies regarding underground water. In its findings the committee stated, "There is no problem in times of plenty, but times of scarcity are likely to become more frequent as population increases. The question here, then, is whether type of use should be the prime basis for a water right, leaving priority of use as determinative only among those using water for a similar purpose."[14] The committee went on to state that, if type of use is to become a determining factor in allocation, then all consumptive uses should be reviewed, not just domestic and agricultural uses. The committee report concluded that "in order to achieve the maximum development of the available water resources, it may be necessary to modify the present system substantially in some areas."[15]

In recent years this question has been asked about the appropriation doctrine in many western states. "It [the prior appropriation doctrine] does *not* reflect concern that water be allocated equitably, as new conditions develop. . . . What we really need is an equitable system of reallocating existing rights—one that implicitly shows greater concern for community values, our children's future, and our degraded environment."[16]

The question of scarcity allocation is important to Utah groundwater, because over 60 percent of the population depends on groundwater for domestic supplies, with seventeen counties "almost entirely dependent" on groundwater as the sole drinking water source.[17] In recent years dependence on groundwater has increased dramatically, primarily due to the extended drought. In 1990 groundwater withdrawals totaled 910,000 acre-feet, which was 53,000 acre-feet more than the previous year and 162,000 acre-feet more than the average withdrawal for the previous decade.[18]

Although structural solutions have been the primary means of supplying a growing demand for water in Utah, at some point in the future, if population and economic growth continue, the legal questions of scarcity and priorities within the definition of beneficial use will surely arise. At that point the application of the prior appropriation doctrine to groundwater within the state may be significantly modified.

One method for expanding the availability of groundwater in the state is aquifer recharge.[19] This entails pumping surplus surface water into the ground, so that it can later be extracted when needed. Currently, one demonstration project in the Salt Lake Valley, administered by the Salt Lake County Water

Conservancy District, is testing the feasibility of this technique. In response to the potential legal challenges that may result from recharge projects, the 1991 legislature passed legislation regulating recharge projects. Senate Bill 71, which became law on April 29, 1991, set basic parameters for recharge projects and assigned specific rulemaking to be administratively handled in the office of the state engineer via a permit system.[20]

In regard to recharge permits, section 202 establishes four parameters: first, the project must not result in unreasonable harm to land or vested water rights; second, the applicant must have the technical and financial capacity to carry out the project; third, the applicant must hold valid, existing rights to the recharge water; and fourth, a water quality permit must be obtained. Each of these requirements raises questions that may be addressed through the courts or result in a political challenge at some time in the future. An examination of each parameter reveals how such challenges might result.

Damage to existing property could result from recharge projects if the aquifer head (the highest point of water in the aquifer) is raised enough to force artesian wells that are dry at the current level of the aquifer to begin flowing again. If a long-forgotten artesian well or spring begins to flow in a developed commercial or residential area, damage could be significant. A more disastrous result might occur from the fact that "plugging of artificially recharged aquifers by biological growth is a serious problem and is frequently a limiting factor in the success of artificial recharge operations."[21] The legal and political results of plugging an aquifer or a major recharge area (such as the mouth of Little Cottonwood Canyon, where the current demonstration project is taking place) would be profound.

The state engineer, whose job is to prevent such catastrophes, will take reasonable precautions to prevent such an occurrence, but if those precautions require that recharge water be of equal or higher quality to naturally occurring recharge waters, then aquifer recharge may be unfeasible in areas such as the canyons east of the Wasatch Front. Water for the current demonstration project comes from Deer Creek Reservoir, where algal growth is much higher than in water naturally occurring in Little Cottonwood Canyon. "Plugging of the aquifer is our biggest concern," according to Richard Bay, chief engineer for the Salt Lake County Water Conservancy District and project manager for the current recharge demonstration project.[22] There is at least some potential for aquifer plugging, and the state engineer will be forced to balance the social and economic good that may result against the political and legal ramifications of a failed project. "Ultimately, tradeoffs may be made 'for the greater public benefit' between [underground] reservoir development and established private uses and prior rights."[23]

The second parameter requires the technical and financial capacity of the recharge applicant to be sufficient to complete the project. At question is whether the applicant will also be required to have the technical and financial capacity to correct any potential detrimental results, such as those described above. If this qualification is included, then recharge projects may be unfeasible in many cases. Given these constraints, the state engineer may apply relaxed standards if the potential societal benefit is large enough to assume the concomitant risks.

The third parameter requires that the applicant have current, valid rights to the recharge water. One legal question that might arise is that of beneficial use. Specifically at question is that portion of the recharge water that may not be recaptured. "The amount of recovery can be predicted if the properties of the aquifer and hydraulic systems are known or measured,"[24] but a question of beneficial use versus waste might be legally challenged if the recapture is anything less than 100 percent. While commingling of waters is legally acceptable,[25] no case law covering recharge exists in Utah at this time.[26] Thus the question of whether aquifer recharge constitutes beneficial use is not addressed in the legislation, because "the Legislature chooses to approach the question of beneficial use by not defining what is beneficial use but only by defining what it is not."[27] Waste has not been traditionally viewed as beneficial use, and appropriators wasting water have usually lost their rights to that wasted water. In a time of critical scarcity, any "waste" of water may be challenged.

The fourth parameter specifically relates to water quality. The Utah Department of Environmental Health has issued an underground injection control (UIC) permit for the current recharge demonstration project because the project, utilizes a well injection system for recharge water. The UIC permit allows the project at least partially to circumvent the protection levels established in section 4.3 of the State of Utah Ground Water Quality Protection Regulations. This is because discharges to groundwater under a UIC permit are not held to as strict a standard as discharges to groundwater under a standard groundwater discharge permit. The political implication here is that the Division of Environmental Health might apply different standards to different permit applicants for similar projects.

The application of the numerical standards and protection levels specified in the state Ground Water Quality Protection Regulations to the recharge water quality in the current demonstration project shows that the levels of chromium, lead, and total dissolved solids all exceed the levels allowable under a standard discharge permit.[28] However, because a UIC permit was issued for this project, the Ground Water Quality Protection Regulations allow the project to fall under regulation R-448-6-6.2, "Permit by Rule," by which the recharge water may contain up to the maximum (numerical) contaminant value listed in the quality standards, and total dissolved solids are limited by the class limitation, which is 500 mg/l in this case. There is no evidence that the Division of Environmental Health consciously made the decision to circumvent its own guidelines. Rather, it appears from discussions with division personnel that the permit procedure was in place utilizing the UIC system, while the Ground Water Quality Protection Regulations do not specifically deal with recharge injection projects. The purpose of this discussion has not been to indict the system, but only to demonstrate how different standards could apply to similar projects in the future.

The preceding discussion of underground water quantity in Utah has dealt with available supplies, the current legal status of access to groundwater, and areas where significant future political and legal controversies might be expected. Information presented in this discussion of quantity indicates that the changing use of groundwater from agricultural to public supply will likely result in a modified view of the traditional allocation system of prior appropriation so that type of use may gain a level of priority not previously attained. The political and legal battles required to make these changes will likely pit rural (agricultural) interests against urban (municipal public supply) interests, a conflict the state legislature has rigorously avoided in the past.[29]

Agricultural appropriators of groundwater will vigorously defend their historical rights under the prior appropriation doctrine, but two factors will work against the traditional system. First, the contribution of agriculture to the state's economy has been decreasing for several decades. And second, the population of the state continues to shift from rural to urban and suburban. These factors will decrease the level of influence the agricultural industry has traditionally held in state politics.

Although case law has not dealt with these changes, state statutes provide an avenue for challenges to the traditional dominance of agriculture in groundwater appropriation. Other interest groups, including industry, mining, and environmental organizations, will also be players in these conflicts over quantity, as each group attempts to include its own priorities in a changing legal and political arena. This discussion of quantity has revolved around future controversy, but a review of current groundwater quality issues, the subject of the next section, shows that conflict among affected interest groups has already begun.

Groundwater Quality Issues

Groundwater policymaking can be very contentious. Because of the close physical ties between groundwater quality and land use activities, pollution control measures may affect several different constituencies with political clout in state capitals. In no other environmental policy arena is a more diverse set of vested interests—agriculture, industry, residential home owners, local government—potentially affected by the outcome of the decision-making process.[30]

Concomitant with the in-state political difficulties of groundwater quality legislation is the potential for state-federal conflicts over primacy in groundwater quality control.[31] In addition to the vested interests listed above, numerous environmental and citizen groups are directly involved with groundwater quality issues.

Public concern about groundwater contamination is not new. Contaminated well water was thought to be the cause of the Black Death by some in medieval Europe.[32] Robert Gottlieb notes, "The search for additional water supplies in the early days of the republic was also a search for a safe water source. Many of the wells inside the city limits of places like Boston and Philadelphia were contaminated from the poor and rapidly declining sanitary conditions in the new urban centers."[33]

Groundwater quality discussions in Utah are also not new. The 1955 Three Citizen Committee's report indicated that existing quality must be known before effective administration of groundwater could take place.[34] However, it was not until 1984 that the governor issued an Executive Order calling for a state groundwater protection strategy.[35] This was the first significant effort to protect the state's groundwater resource.

The governor's executive order was a response to growing concern, both nationally and at the state level, over increasing groundwater contamination. Nationally, Love Canal, Times Beach, Woburn (Massachusetts), and other contaminated community groundwater drinking supplies were discovered, debated, and litigated. Utah also has potentially serious groundwater contamination problems: "Currently, eleven hazardous-waste sites in Utah are on the CERCLA [Superfund] National Priority List with 2 additional sites being proposed and are registered under CERCLA by the Utah Division of Enviromental Response and Remediation. Eleven of these sites are known to have groundwater contamination problems."[36] A review of some of the conflicts over water quality in the state reveals the political maneuvering of state government, industry, and other interest groups in response to this newly perceived problem.

Public Awareness and Governmental Response

In a November 23, 1975, *Salt Lake Tribune* article, then Utah County Commissioner Yuke Inouye stated that "the biggest problem in Utah County is the threat of underground water pollution."[37] Commissioner Inouye's statement was in response to groundwater pollution occurring under two county landfills, one in Spanish Fork and the other just north of the Geneva Steel plant. "We are being watched closely by EPA and have been given three years to find solutions to the problems we have," said Inouye. Two aspects of his statements are important for the development of groundwater protection programs in the state. First, there is an implicit acknowledgment that government activities are intimately involved in groundwater pollution problems, both as a regulator and as a direct cause in this case. The second important aspect is the developing federal-state relationship in groundwater protection. The EPA, not quite five years old at that time, had come into Utah with a big stick, at least according to Inouye.

In 1980 the U.S. Geological Survey investigated whether groundwater pollution had occurred in the southwestern portion of the Salt Lake Valley. Mining activities of the Kennecott Copper Corporation at the Bingham open-pit mine had been suspected as a cause of the pollution for several years. The Geological Survey's findings, reported by UPI writer E. O'Neil Robinson, were that "pollutants leached from Kennecott's mining operations in Salt Lake City and from natural ore deposits have been contaminating the Salt Lake Valley underground water since at least 1969."[38] One other statement in the article is important to the overall discussion of water in Utah: "Central Utah Project officials recently cited the polluted wells of the western Salt Lake Valley as one reason CUP is needed to provide culinary water supplies for the expanding population." Finger pointing in Utah had begun. The state's groundwater pollution problems were being presented to a national audience and were being used to justify other governmental activities.

By late 1980, possible links between groundwater contamination and public health problems were being investigated. When a seemingly high number of miscarriages occurred in Kearns (a suburb of Salt Lake City), groundwater that had previously been identified as contaminated by Kennecott's mining operation was cited by local residents as a possible cause. County, state, and federal government officials were quick to discount any connection and blamed "rumors and misinformation for the concern in the subdivision."[39] Water quality tests in the area showed nothing unusual, but a study of the spontaneous abortions had not been completed when the story was published in the *Salt Lake Tribune*. Ken Harris, an environmental health specialist with the state Bureau of Water Supplies, is quoted in the same article: "But the people out there don't realize that they aren't drinking the groundwater . . . the water they drink comes from deep wells located quite a bit farther east." Harris did not report that the aquifer downgradient in that part of the valley is to the east.

The EPA's position was stated by Dr. Jim Baker, environmental health specialist with the EPA in Denver: "Frankly, it looks like some activist group out there got hold of some statistics and used them inappropriately."[40] Terry Sadler, director of environmental health for the Salt Lake City–County Health Department, had a slightly different view of the controversy: "This sort of thing happens three or four times a year. . . . Women get together and hear that so-and-so had a miscarriage, and they just had one, and they become concerned. And, of course, the first thing they look to in rationalizing the incident is their environment."[41] The controversy subsided, at least in the media, but it heightened awareness of the potential dangers of groundwater pollution. The state began developing a groundwater protection policy.

By 1986, as a result of the governor's executive order, a protection strategy for the state's groundwater had been established by the Utah Water Pollution Control Committee. The strategy was not without controversy, however. *Deseret News* environmental specialist Joseph M. Bauman reported that the only two citizen representatives on the committee were representatives of the Utah Industry Environmental Coalition. "The Industry Environmental Coalition is actually a group of companies including Kennecott, Utah Power & Light, Hercules, Western Zirconium and Morton-Thiokol. Some of them have severe groundwater pollution problems," wrote Bauman. He reported that Robert P. Barnes, groundwater geologist for the Bureau of Water Pollution Control, explained that there were no environmental interests represented on the committee because, "The problem is finding [environmental] people on any consistent basis. . . . You look at the report, judge it on its merits, and show me where the bias exists. I don't think it does."[42]

A review of activities exempted in the Ground Water Quality Protection Regulations does identify at least one area where industry participation in the development of the regulations may have resulted in a partial exemption for that industry. Section R 448-6-6.2.6 exempts the regulations from pollution caused by "natural groundwater seeping or flowing into conventional mine workings which re-enters the ground by natural gravity flow prior to pumping or transporting out of the mine and without being in any mining or metallurgical process." According to Ralf Bohn, environmental health scientist with the Bureau of Water Pollution Control, mine waters were excluded because the bureau is waiting for federal legislation to provide standards and guidance in developing pollution controls for this activity.[43] Robert Barnes reiterated the reason no conservationists were involved with the development of the regulations: none came forward and wanted to be involved.[44]

In 1987 the connection between mining in the western part of the valley and groundwater contamination was still being denied. Kenneth Bousfield, Utah's chief compliance officer for drinking water safety, claimed that even though "Several private wells were taken out of service because they were within areas of groundwater contamination. . . . The contamination could be from a natural cause; it may be enhanced by [mining] activities."[45] But by 1988 a direct connection between mining and groundwater contamination was admitted by British Petroleum, then the owner of the Kennecott mine and facilities.[46]

On August 14, 1989, the Ground Water Quality Protection Regulations went into effect.[47] Within three months their effectiveness was being challenged, this time by a member of the scientific community. "If what has been allowed to happen near Geneva Steel in Utah County is indicative of how the state is enforcing groundwater standards, the state could be in serious trouble."[48] BYU biologist Paul Evans explained that well water near the Geneva Steel facility, which had met groundwater quality standards prior to 1986, exceeded the standard for benzene by fifteen hundred times.[49]

"Some 'environmentalists' accord themselves a higher plane of existence than the rest of us," said Robert Barnes during an interview. "They don't understand that most of us involved are trying to deal with these problems in the best way we can."[50] Barnes was concerned that some environmentalists don't understand, or don't want to understand, the legal complexities and rules that must be followed for environmental change to take place. One issue where environmental groups differ significantly with state officials concerns federal versus state primacy over groundwater protection.

On June 24, 1988, a coalition of environmental groups, including the Environmental Defense Fund, the National Wildlife Federation, the Audubon Society, and others, presented *Protecting the Nation's Groundwater: A Proposal for Federal Legislation* to members of Congress. Such legislation had already been introduced earlier in the session (Senate bills 20 and 1105 and House Resolution 791). These bills would have shifted the existing level of state primacy toward a much higher level of involvement and control by the federal government. Essentially they called for the EPA to set specific numerical standards for groundwater contaminants and to establish firm timetables that all states would be required to meet in developing programs to meet those standards.

The state of Utah, through several political channels, expressed its opposition to any shift away from state primacy. The Utah State Legislature, in a joint resolution, urged "Congress in its consideration of national groundwater policy to assure that any legislation that is enacted is faithful to and supportive of the primary role and responsibility of states in managing groundwater."[51] The Western Regional Council, a group consisting of the chief executive officers of many private western companies and public utilities, provided testimony in support of the state's position during hearings on the bills: "The WRC, however, does not believe legislation creating a comprehensive Federal groundwater regulatory program is necessary or appropriate. The basic responsibility and authority for groundwater management should remain with the States." The Western States Water Council (WSWC), a research and lobbying group appointed by sixteen western governors and funded by those sixteen western states, also provided testimony at the hearings: "There is widespread agreement that the States should continue to have the exclusive responsibility with regard to the creation and administration of groundwater rights.[52]

In a 1989 letter from Rebecca W. Hanmer, acting assistant administrator for water, EPA, to D. Craig Bell, WSWC executive director, the traditional position of state primacy was acknowledged by the EPA, which recognized "the need for flexibility to develop programs appropriate to a state's circumstances, enhancement of federal technical assistance to states, and availability of federal funds to assist states in implementation as well as program development."[53] Norman Johnson, legal counsel for the WSWC, stated that a state-federal battle over groundwater may be on the horizon.[54] The states are resisting an EPA position regarding state primacy expressed in the 1990 *EPA Groundwater Task Force Report.*[55] That report noted that the agency's role may grow as new contaminants are identified and numerical levels are established.

Whether there will actually be a shift to federal controls over groundwater pollution remains to be seen, especially in light of the Republican takeover of Congress in 1994. Nevertheless, the Clinton administration may attempt to increase federal control over groundwater in those states where there is a widespread perception that state administration is clearly inadequate. In 1994 the U.S. Congress attempted to reauthorize both the Clean Water Act and the "Superfund" law (CERCLA), but failed. These issues will undoubtedly arise again in the 104th Congress, and the debate promises to be quite contentious.[56] This in turn could directly affect groundwater policy in Utah.

Conclusion

This analysis of the politics of groundwater in Utah has focused on two primary topics: quantity and quality. The discussion of quantity is concerned with application of existing statutes to a changing demand structure. At question in the future will be the definition of scarcity, priorities among different beneficial uses, and management of evolving technologies such as aquifer recharge. Future controversies are likely to be intense as challenges to traditional rights and uses are raised.

Regulation of groundwater quality in Utah has experienced significant changes in the past few years. Special interest groups have had some success in promoting their own priorities, while the news media have heightened public concern and involvement in these issues. An educational outreach program has been established by the Utah Division of Water Quality. Continuing change is the prognosis for quality control regulations in the future. Increasing numbers of contaminants will be regulated and competing interest groups will continue to promote their own priorities.

Notes

1. See Zachary Smith, *Groundwater in the West* (San Diego: Academic Press, 1990); Henry Kenski, *Saving the Hidden Treasure* (Claremont, CA: Regina Books, 1990); John Redifer and Sandra Davis, "Implementing Groundwater Policy: Contaminating the Message," paper prepared for delivery at the 1993 Annual Meeting of the Western Political Science Association, Pasadena, Calif., March 18–20, 1993.

2. "Estimated Use of Water in the United States in 1990," U. S. Geological Survey, Circular no. 1081 (Washington, D.C., 1993), p. 17.

3. Don Price, "Ground Water in Utah's Densely Populated Wasatch Front Area: The Challenges and the Choices" (Washington, D.C.: U.S. Geological Survey, 1985), p. 2.

4. Ibid., p. 57; and L. R. Herbert, et al., "Ground-Water Conditions in Utah, Spring of 1990," Cooperative Investigations Report no. 30, U.S. Geological Survey and Utah Divisions of Water Resources and Water Rights (Salt Lake City, 1990).

5. A. G. Hely, et al., "Water Resources of Salt Lake County, Utah," Utah Department of Natural Resources, Technical Publication 31 (Salt Lake City, 1971), table 21.

6. Marc Reisner and Sarah Bates, *Overtapped Oasis: Reform or Revolution for Western Water* (Washington, D.C.: Island Press, 1990), p. 100.

7. Utah Code Annotated, p. 49.

8. David H. Getches, *Water Law in a Nutshell*, 2d ed. (St. Paul, Minn: West Publishing Co., 1990), p. 426.

9. *Riordan v. Westwood* (115 Utah 215, 203, 1949), P.2nd 922.

10. State Water Plan Coordinating Committee, *Utah State Water Plan* (Salt Lake City, 1990), sec. 5.2.

11. Utah Code 73-3-21.

12. Utah Department of Natural Resources, *Achievements* (Salt Lake City, 1970), p. 1.

13. State Water Plan Coord. Comm., *Utah State Water Plan* (1990), sec. 4.4.

14. Three Citizen Committee, *A Study of Water Administration, Underground*

Water Resource Management, and Flood Water Control in Utah (Salt Lake City, October 1956), p. 15.

15. Ibid., p. 22.

16. Reisner and Bates, *Overtapped Oasis*, p. 65.

17. Utah Division of Water Quality and League of Women Voters of Salt Lake, "Local Ground Water Protection," brochure produced as a part of a Groundwater Protection Community Education Project (Salt Lake City, [1993]). Also see Kidd M. Waddell and Marvin H. Maxwell, "Utah Ground-Water Quality," *National Water Summary, 1986*, U.S. Geological Survey Water-Supply Paper 2325 (Washington, D.C., 1988), p. 493.

18. U.S. Geological Survey, "Groundwater Conditions in Utah, Spring, 1991," Cooperative Investigations Report no. 31, (Division of Water Resources, Utah Department of Natural Resources, Salt Lake City, 1991). The 1991–92 "Annual Report" of the Salt Lake City Department of Public Utilities, p. 2, notes that the city's eighteen deep wells are dropping between 2 and 5 feet a year.

19. Richard P. Bay and Steven Bowser, "Operating Experience with the Southeast Salt Lake County Artificial Groundwater Recharge Demonstration Project," paper presented to the Artificial Recharge of Groundwater Symposium, Tucson, Ariz., May 19–21, 1993.

20. The Groundwater Recharge and Recovery Act, 73-3b-101-106, effective April 29, 1991.

21. Warren W. Wood, "Toward a Rational Development of Artificial Recharge," in Z. Saleem, ed., *Advances in Groundwater Hydrology* (Minneapolis, Minn.: American Water Resources Association, 1976), p. 245.

22. Richard Bay, telephone interview, November 30, 1990.

23. State Water Plan Coord. Comm., *Utah State Water Plan* (1990), sec. 19.2.1.

24. Wood, "Rational Development of Artificial Recharge," p. 244.

25. Utah Code Annotated, Title 73, sec. 3-20.

26. Bay, interview.

27. Jeanenne Larson, telephone interview, November 28, 1990.

28. Salt Lake County Water Conservancy District, *Phase II Project Development Plan for the Southeast Salt Lake County Artificial Groundwater Recharge Demonstration Project* (Salt Lake City, January 1990), table VI-I.

29. Larson, interview.

30. Larry Morandi, *State Groundwater Protection Policies: A Legislator's Guide* (Denver, Colo./Washington, D.C.: National Conference of State Legislators, 1989).

31. See U.S. General Accounting Office, "Groundwater Protection: The Use of Drinking Water Standards by the States," report to the chairman, Subcommittee on Hazardous Wastes and Toxic Substances, Committee on Environmental and Public Works, U.S. Senate, GAO/PEMD-89-1 (Washington, D.C., December 1988).

32. Robert S. Gottfried, *The Black Death: Natural and Human Disaster in Medieval Europe* (New York: The Free Press, 1983), p. 52.

33. Robert Gottlieb, *A Life of Its Own: The Politics and Power of Water* (New York: Harcourt Brace Jovanovich, 1988), p. 159.

34. Three Citizen Committee, A *Study of Water Administration*, p. 12.

35. Utah Bureau of Water Pollution Control, *State of Utah Ground Water Quality Protection Regulations* (Salt Lake City, 1989), sec. 1.2.

36. Utah Division of Water Quality, Department of Environmental Quality, *State of Utah Water Quality Assessment for 1992*, Section 305(b) Report (Salt Lake City, August 1992), p. 52.

37. R. C. Roberg, "Utah County Moves a Step Closer to Ending Solid Waste Problem," *Salt Lake Tribune*, November 23, 1975, p. C-1.

38. O'Neil Robinson, "Study Says Mining, Ore Deposits Pollute Water," *Deseret News*, July 4, 1980, p. B-1.

39. Mike Carter, "Subdivision Water-Abortion Link Denied," *Salt Lake Tribune*, November 11, 1980, pp. B-1, B-3.

40. Ibid.

41. Ibid.

42. Joseph M. Bauman, "Utah Groundwater Study Lacked Input of Conservationists, *Deseret News*, November 28, 1986, p. A-11.

43. Ralf Bohn, telephone interview, November 30, 1990.

44. Robert P. Barnes, interview, December 3, 1990.

45. "Extent of Water Pollution Studied," *Deseret News*, November 11, 1987, p. D-1.

46. Jim Woolf, "BP Minerals' Efforts Diluting Groundwater Problems," *Salt Lake Tribune*, June 4, 1988, p. B-1.

47. R317-7, Utah Administrative Code, Administrative Rules for Groundwater Quality Protection, codified February 10, 1990.

48. "Geneva Wells May Portend Larger Problem," *Deseret News*, November 6, 1989, p. A-10.

49. Ibid.

50. Barnes, interview.

51. U.S. Senate Committee on Environment and Public Works, Subcommittee on Water Resources, Transportation, and Infrastructure, *Ground Water Protection: Joint Hearings before the Subcommittees on Water Resources, Transportation, and Infrastructure, and Hazardous Wastes and Toxic Substances of the Committee on Environment and Public Works*, 100th Congress, 2d session, on S. 20, S. 1105, and H.R. 791 (February 23, March 24, and May 17, 1988).

52. Ibid. The Western States Water Council is headquartered in Salt Lake City.

53. Rebecca W. Hanmer to D. Craig Bell, September 18, 1989.

54. Norman Johnson, interview, November 28, 1990.

55. Environmental Protection Agency, *Ground-Water Task Force Report*, draft final (Washington, D.C., September 27, 1990).

56. See "Complexities Face Congress in 'Superfund' Overhaul," *CQ Weekly Report* (February 5, 1994): 239–40; and "Debate on Clean Water Act Echoes States' Fears," *CQ Weekly Report* (February 5, 1994): 242–43.

CHAPTER SEVEN

The Politics of Instream Flow

Ann Wechsler

The concept of instream flow, the flow required to maintain the ecological integrity of a stream, is relatively recent. Prior to the 1970s, "minimum streamflows," defined as a flow level below which fish cannot survive, were secured by state and federal fishery agencies for the protection of fish alone. As a general goal, however, minimum flow had serious deficiencies.[1] Chief among them was the assumption that if the needs of fish are met, the needs of riparian vegetation would also be met. It is now widely accepted that if habitat and cover for fish are compromised for a period of time, fish will also be affected.[2] A more effective standard bases the flow requirements on the resource with the greatest water need, "otherwise the system could degrade, given the interdependency of ecosystem components."[3] The term "instream flow" is now generally accepted to mean a stream flow that will satisfy the needs of aquatic resources in addition to fish, as well as the riparian zone dependent upon the stream flow.

This chapter focuses on instream flow in Utah. Many western states have enacted laws recognizing instream flow for recreational use and/or wildlife maintenance. Maintaining a given flow between two points on a stream (but not at the point of diversion) is recognized by Alaska, Arizona, Colorado, Idaho, Montana, Nevada, Oregon, Wyoming, and Utah.[4] Utah law recognizes the transfer of existing rights to accommodate instream flow for limited uses,[5] as do Colorado, Wyoming, and Oregon,[6] but it does not permit the filing of new appropriations for instream flows.[7]

One of the reasons Utah lacks water laws conducive to instream flow uses is that the state has little if any unappropriated water. "In 1972, the Utah State Division of Water Resources estimated that the existing demand for water resources in Utah greatly exceeds the current supply of water. More applications for appropriations of water are presently filed with the state engineer's office than can be approved without exceeding the total available supply of water in the state."[8] Development of other resources, such as coal and tar sands, were expected to place additional demands on Utah's water supply.[9] States that have a great deal of unappropriated water and a recognition of the economic value of water left in a stream are less hesitant to implement instream flows.[10] However, in a state where the water supply is already appropriated, as is the case in Utah, establishing instream flows is not an easy task.

The present tension over instream flow in Utah is between those who have acquired or seek to acquire water from streams for traditional use and those who seek to maintain stream flows adequate to support various life forms or recreational activities. The prior appropriation doctrine has historically supported consumptive diversions of stream flows, which in the past has proved detrimental to nonconsumptive uses. In the mid-1980s, the Division of Wildlife Resources was granted an instream flow right, but not to allocate new waters, and only for the propagation of fish.[11]

Recent data from the Utah Division of Wildlife Resources of the Department of Natural Resources, indicates that 53 percent of the state's 6,200 miles of stream fisheries "suffer moderate to total losses of fishery potential annually by dewatering."[12] Of the affected miles of streams, more than half lose from 60 percent to 100 percent of their natural flow by diversion.[13] In the southwest corner of the state alone, rapid growth in the past two decades has led to closures of groundwater basins and limitations on the appropriation of surface water. Since 1980 the population has increased by 50 percent in this region;[14] this growth, coupled with proposals for hydroelectric projects in the area, increase the probability that more streams will be dewatered at least for short reaches.

Scarcity of water amid increasing growth (both of population and of industry) is one factor that siphons water from its natural channels; economic value placed on the diversion of water from streams is another. Historically, mining and agricultural interests caused the greatest pressure on stream flows.[15] These interests were followed by the burgeoning municipalities, which placed a strong value on pure drinking water. Intermittent drought in the Great Basin has always led to great concern for water shortages, and impoundments have resulted. The value placed on use of water outside the stream channel is, as a result of the threat of shortages, pervasive in the state.

However, we are beginning to witness a shift in values and an evolution in water law to recognize instream flows. There are many who place increasing importance on recreational opportunities, wildlife preservation,[16] the spiritual values associated with free-flowing water,[17] and "existence value"—the benefits derived from knowing that unique areas are protected, even if one never plans to visit them. For those who do plan to visit the area at some future date, this water represents an option value.[18] The aesthetic value of stream flow, the contribution of free-flowing water to quality of life whether put to use or not, and preservation of the natural world as being healthier and safer for people, are themes that occur more frequently in our society. The issues of health and safety are also relevant to instream flows. Current agricultural practices are a major source of nonpoint water pollution (water that does not reach a stream by a discrete conveyance) in forty-five states and territories. In the affected river stretches, lakes, and estuarine areas, agriculture is identified as the primary source of pollutants in 64 percent, 57 percent, and 19 percent of these water bodies, respectively. The pollutants are mainly sediments, but they also include nitrogen and phosphorus from agricultural fertilizers, pesticides, and salts and minerals that make their way back to stream channels through irrigation runoff.[19]

Accompanying these changes in values and preferences is a concomitant change in the makeup of political pressure groups and the tactics employed to promote instream uses. It is this additional demand for allocation of an already scarce resource, clean water, that has led to conflict, and it is quite likely that water disputes will dominate the political agenda in the West in the coming years.

Five Factors Affecting Instream Flow Policy

To understand the instream flow issue, it is necessary to explore economic, technical, administrative, legal, and political factors.

Economic Factors

Instream flow negotiations are often driven by economics, and consequently much attention has been given to this aspect of instream flow in the literature. Those who favor protection of stream flows tend to stress the economic benefits that are derived compared to offstream uses, whereas others employ similar comparisons to opposite ends. Economic figures from the Utah Division of Wildlife Resources indicate that there is a high economic value placed on wildlife-related activities, commercial boating, and fishing in Utah. The 1990 *State Water Plan* reports almost 500,000 Utahns engaged in fishing and 207,000 in hunting.[20] They contributed more than $276 million to Utah's economy in 1985. Nonconsumptive wildlife pursuits generated $120 million. Economist Bonnie Colby goes a step further in her analysis of the dollar value placed on recreation, water quality, and nonuser values. She suggests that "the economic value of instream flows can be measured so as to be comparable to the value in offstream uses such as irrigation. Instream values can be equal to or greater than water values in many consumptive uses, especially in important recreation and wildlife areas."[21] Marc Reisner and Sarah Bates state that there is increasing evidence that water left in streams or used to sustain wetlands is of greater economic value than that used to irrigate certain crops.[22] In western states opinion polls indicate strong public support for more fish and wildlife habitat and hence greater instream flows. However, a substantial shift in policy will require compelling economic studies as well as a legal and institutional framework that will foster change. Even more important may be the need to change traditionally hostile attitudes toward reserving water in streams for environmental pur-poses.[23]

Technical Factors

How much stream flow to dedicate to the propagation of fish, the watering of stock, or anything else that is normally associated with flowing water is, ultimately, dependent upon answers to technical problems. Methodologies for quantifying stream flow, calculations, and data abound in the literature.

It was not, however, until instream flow had acquired some legitimacy, as seen by the passage of statutes in recent decades, that methods for determining water requirements for instream uses were developed. B. L. Lamb and A. R. Doerksen have divided instream flow methodologies into two groups: those designed for preliminary planning and those methodologies for the evaluation of impacts from a project. The preliminary planning methods "typically use a streamflow characteristic that represents the minimum flow for a particular instream use."[24] Impact assessments use incremental methods to estimate the quality of fish habitats at different increments of stream flow. "Early investigators . . . used depth velocity, and substrate criteria to evaluate the influence of incremental changes in streamflow on the quality of spawning habitat for salmon in Washington streams."[25] Given an established methodology, the specific technique used will depend on several factors, including management policy, geographic region, and species.

These physical models are vital to instream flow evaluation, but the administrative, legal, and political arenas will have the greatest impact on the future of our streams; and it is in these areas that the greatest potential for divisiveness occurs.

Administrative Factors

The administrative apparatus for acquiring water rights in Utah is defined by statute. The water right transfer process is based on the prior appropriation doctrine and is administered

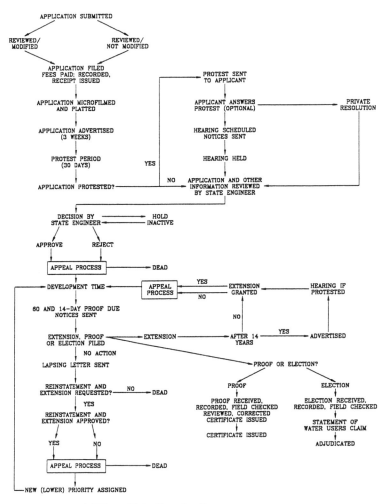

Figure 7.1. Utah Water Right Transfer Process

through the State Engineer's Office by a permitting process (see Fig. 7.1).[26] When the process is complete, the water user holds a vested right which is considered a form of real property, and is transferable.

Two types of formal transfer are the "change" and "exchange" amendments. The former refers to a change in the point of diversion, place of use, and/or nature of use of a water right; the latter contains a contractual agreement between two or more water users. Both require approval of the state engineer. An informal exchange is the exchange of water shares within mutual irrigation companies or within water districts; the exchange remains inside the designated boundaries of the company or the district, and the legally defined use does not change. Therefore, informal exchanges are not monitored by the state engineer.

Water rights transactions in Utah have been proceeding swiftly over the past two decades. Between 1975 and 1987, there were 6,493 "change" applications, and 1,721 "exchange applications."[27] Water transfers are important, according to law professor Ray Jay Davis, because they "are a key to successful water resources management which is essential to Utah's economic well-being."[28] His analysis of transfer activity led him to the conclusion that the high volume of water rights sales, exchanges, and leases "demonstrates that the state code has not thwarted operation of a water rights transfer system."[29] The state engineer has the authority to curtail exchanges when rapid development occurs, as it did in the Snyderville Basin prior to 1981, coupled with insufficient hydrologic data.[30]

Another party with legal authority to engage in water rights transfers has recently appeared on the scene. In 1986 the Division of Wildlife Resources (DWR) was given the right by the Utah legislature to file change applications respecting: "1) perfected water rights already owned by the division; 2) perfected water rights purchased by that division through funding provided for that purpose by the legislature, or acquired by lease, exchange or gift; or 3) appurtenant water rights acquired through buying real estate for other wildlife purposes".[31] The purpose of this amendment was to grant the DWR the capacity to obtain water rights to protect fish. The specific purpose must be indicated in the change application. However, for any long-term change, the agency must get legislative approval, a stipulation that brings many political factors into the change application process.

As discussed above, securing instream flows requires the technical capability for quantifying the flows needed for various identified resources. It also requires the administrative capability to deliver flows based on statutory provisions. The actual delivery of sufficient water to a stream can, however, be much more complex. In land management issues, the planning process, which includes ample provisions for gauging public sentiment, has been tested through twenty-one years of implementation of the National Environmental Policy Act. In contrast, the prior appropriation doctrine has not served the streams very well (most stream dewatering took place before the turn of the century). Thus a truly equitable water allocation system is in its infancy. We have the technical capability to quantify instream flows, but the expression of values associated with recreation and leisure-time activities is not easily applied. Instream flow determinations would benefit from "an approach that recognizes and thoroughly delineates resource values," predicated upon an interdisciplinary, value-based approach that recognizes competing resource values. [32]

Once resource values have been acknowledged, the administrative structure should have the flexibility to deliver the appropriate amount of water for that use. A team-based evaluation process (including specialists representing hydrology/hydraulics, geomorphology, and law) would permit maximum flexibility as well as greater sensitivity to the entire ecosystem. Such an approach to instream flow determinations would combine both administrative and technical considerations.

As the complexity of the process increases, however, so does the opportunity for political input. The administrative apparatus pertinent to instream flow is closely tied to the legal framework; state statutes can either facilitate or inhibit instream flow appropriations.

Legal Factors

The appropriation doctrine, with its two main principles—beneficial use and a hierarchical structure based on time of diversion—has permitted the overappropriation of natural flowing streams, even though there may be underappropriation during periods of high flow. In spite of natural fluctuations between high and low flows, making it difficult to determine how much of a stream should be left intact, emerging interest groups have put forth new claims, increasing the competition for a share of instream flows. The new groups on the scene include sports enthusiasts (engaged in both fishing and hunting), commercial and noncommercial rafters, wilderness and fish and wildlife advocates, landowning organizations such as the Trust for Public Land and the Nature Conservancy, and municipalities.[33]

The public trust doctrine implies different things to different people, but "the notion that instream flows may be protected by the public trust arises from the growing body of case law holding that streams, lakes, marshlands, and other water resources are part of the people's heritage, and that the state has both the authority and the duty to protect those resources."[34] In California students concerned over the deleterious effects of long-term water diversions on Mono Lake organized the Mono Lake Committee, which invoked the public trust doctrine in its case to challenge these water diversions. The significance of the case is that the public trust doctrine can serve, in the right circumstances, to limit the amount of water that can be diverted from a public resource.[35]

Utah water appropriation law explicitly recognizes the public trust doctrine as a tool for allocating water. The elements contained in the law to support this interpretation are: "recognition of a legal right in the general public, enforceability of the right against the government, and the potential for interpretation consistent with contemporary concerns for environmental values . . . provide the basis for a judicial declaration that water is and always has been a public trust asset in Utah."[36]

Two significant cases in the Great Basin in which public interest was a factor were *Bonham v. Morgan*,[37] and *Nevada v. Morros*.[38] In the first case, the plaintiff Bonham protested a change application filed by the Salt Lake County Water Conservancy District and Draper Irrigation Co., which sought to change the point of diversion, place, and nature of use of certain water rights. Bonham sustained substantial flooding, which he claimed was the result of the construction of a screw gate, pipeline, and diversion works after defendants obtained preliminary approval of their change application. The state engineer claimed he was without authority to address Bonham's claims, because he was limited to investigating impairments of *vested* water rights, and the plaintiff was not a water user. In its preliminary holding, the court decided the plaintiffs were "aggrieved persons" and were entitled to a trial. In the final holding, the court ruled that the state engineer "must consider the public interest, in addition to other factors, in determining whether or not to approve an application to permanently change the point of diversion or nature of use of appropriated water."[39]

In the *per curium* decision (a brief was filed by the National Parks and Conservation Association [NPCA] on behalf of the plaintiffs), the court also concluded that the same criteria mandated in the appropriation statute must be applied to the change statute.[40] The law states that the proposed use "must not be detrimental to the public welfare."[41] This is a substantive and not a procedural criterion. The court based its opinion on a point raised in the NPCA brief, which posed the hypothetical situation of an applicant appropriating water for a use that would not injure another person and who subsequently files a change application for a use that would prove detrimental to another or to the public welfare. It would prove detrimental if the court had interpreted the criterion to be procedural, not substantive, and to apply to the first application only.[42]

The significance of this decision is perhaps better understood in the context of a current situation in southern Utah, in which the NPCA and the U.S. National Park Service are protesting a proposed diversion of the Virgin River that would affect Zion National Park. The conservancy district holding the water rights on the river has filed two permanent change applications. "One application seeks to change the point of diversion to construct a 40,000 acre-foot reservoir on the East Fork of the Virgin River upstream of the park boundary. The other application also seeks to change the right of diversion to construct a 10,000 acre-foot reservoir on the North Fork of the Virgin River, again upstream of the park boundary."[43] Both activities would be detrimental to the park and its fisheries, and the NPCA and NPS would have standing to sue under the *Bonham* decision, which makes it impossible for the state engineer to ignore the public interest in the change application.

The other case, recently decided in Nevada, also bolstered the consideration of public interest.[44] The Nevada Supreme Court upheld the right of the United States to appropriate stream flows in the Blue Lakes Wilderness Study Area for fish, wildlife, and recreation, without the traditional requirement of a physical diversion. Thus Nevada joined Colorado and Arizona in recognizing instream flow rights and may even clear the way "for individuals or groups to file applications to attempt to obtain instream flow rights under Nevada law."[45]

In summary, the public trust doctrine may be an ancient doctrine that has been moribund for some time with respect to water law, but it is emerging in contemporary environmental issues to protect resources that are inherently public in nature. The extent to which it will alter water resource allocation is not yet known, but its usefulness as a "structure for inhibiting governmentally sanctioned abuse of public resources is acknowledged."[46] As one author points out:

> Utilitarian market forces provide a powerful and often overwhelming justification for the immediate consumption of resources. Under the appropriative system, a competitive user is justified in believing that if he does not use an available resource, someone else will. The public trust doctrine overcomes these economic incentives by providing a rationale powerful enough to compete with the economic realities of the market.[47]

The Barriers to Instream Flow

This chapter has explored economic, technical, administrative, and legal factors that must be considered in any discussion of instream flow protection in the Great Basin. It has also highlighted some of the key players in the controversy over instream flow. The barriers to instream flow in Utah are largely political. In the words of one water attorney who advocates the protection of stream flows,

> even if you can prove that instream flow makes good economic sense, that keeping water in the stream banks can be translated into dollars for the state, and that its the "right thing" to do, it will still take a tremendous education effort to change the values of those

who control water allocation. It's a "conspiracy of convenience" to maintain the status quo. They have been colonizing the West through stream diversion for irrigation, and they have a powerful lobby to protect the status quo.[48]

This lobby is being challenged by a change in demographics and concomitant representation in the legislature. According to Robert Morgan, Utah state engineer, the legislature is not as representative of agricultural interests as it used to be; in the last reapportionment there was a strong shift to represent the cities. "The Farm Bureau still has a strong lobby, but environmental groups, such as the National Audubon Society, also have effective lobbying."[49] The Audubon Society, on the other hand, while agreeing that interest among conservation groups is improving (enough to hold weekly meetings during the legislative session), maintains that their clout as lobbyists is certainly not on a par with the Farm Bureau's. Interest and dedication among environmental organizations and a cadre of volunteers does not immediately translate into the funding necessary for effective lobbying.[50]

The exact composition of the legislature is less important than the extent to which certain legislators control committees. At present, legislators from rural areas generally have great sway in those committees most likely to deal with water allocations. Because wildlife competes with the Farm Bureau's operations, and the legislature funds the Division of Wildlife Resources, if a legislator opposes a political appointee in the division, it could be the end of that person's job. "The relationship is very tenuous," according to Jodi Williams, a member of the Wildlife Advisory Board to the DWR, representing several Utah counties.[51]

Some successful instream flow negotiations have been conducted in a highly politicized climate. The Provo River, for example, has been made a showcase by the Bureau of Reclamation. Partly in response to the fact that the Provo River is a class I brown trout fishery, considerable pressure has been brought to bear on the Bureau to mitigate the effects of the Jordanelle Dam.[52] During recent drought years especially, the future of the river has been of great concern to the public; the project was more rigorously evaluated than usual in response to pressure during drought years. A previous decision to dedicate 100 cubic feet per second to the river was adjusted to 85 cubic feet per second. The Bureau then needed to come up with the best biologically defensible position for such a reduction between Deer Creek and the Elmsted Diversion, and an environmental impact statement (EIS) was completed.[53]

Although the studies completed under an EIS review are an attempt to gauge the consequences of a particular action, an EIS can have deficiencies. According to one of the Bureau's aquatic biologists who was intimately involved with the study, "The EIS is a cooperative venture with other agencies that must be completed in a limited time frame. There are always areas of risk. Mistakes can be made, especially when studying long-lived species such as the Humpback Chubb or the Colorado Squawfish. The best an EIS can be is a snapshot of the environment—we perform the necessary mitigation [of a project] and then we walk away from it."[54]

Other prime fisheries may not fare so well as the Provo River experiment. High visibility and public outcry would appear to be factors that may contribute to maintaining fisheries, but in their absence, the fate of other prime fisheries is in doubt. For example, a self-sustaining cutthroat fishery may be affected by the Narrows Project, near Price. A closer look at the processes involved in other major proposed water diversions (the Narrows Project, the Virgin River, the Weber River, the Price River, and the Bear River, for example) would yield vital information on the competing demands on stream water uses. Because these projects are in varying stages of development, a detailed study of each might shed some light on the changing values with respect to instream flow. One employee at the DWR commented anonymously that he is encouraged by the level of treatment being given to the environmental impacts of the Bear River Project. Authorization has been given to the DWR to assess environmental impacts; just a few years ago that might not have been the case. But an environmental assessment is just that—an assessment; it does not ensure protection of the resource.

The *State Water Plan* (1990) also recognizes that thousands of fishery streams are partially or seasonally dewatered, seriously affecting fishery and wildlife values.[55] In addition, it states that stream flows are increasingly threatened by reservoir construction, hydroelectric generation, spring development, irrigation and/or municipal-industrial diversions, and stock watering. Nevertheless, its recommendations do not appear commensurate with a serious concern. Project developers are advised to talk to the DWR early in the planning stages to assess stream flow requirements. Developers do consult with the division, but the agency appears to be chronically underfunded.[56] The division is now in the process of completing a full inventory of streams that have instream flow commitments, some of which have been obtained from Federal Energy Regulatory Commission hydropower licensing, and some of which have been obtained through cooperative agreements with the Division of Fish and Wildlife, but the effort has been interrupted by a lack of staff. Thus, although instream flow has become a recognized factor, the ability to implement it is often impaired.

Other legislative controls have impeded the DWR from exercising its mandate to acquire instream flows for the propagation of fish. In the 1986 statute, the legislature effectively asserted control by conditioning a water acquisition on legislative approval. The DWR decided to wait until "we have exactly the right situation to test the administrative process to gain approval for its application."[57] "We don't want to fail the first time on some technicality. We have to walk a fine line—not step on toes—to be effective managers and get our programs through . . . but the ball is in our court and we have to test the legislation."[58] The DWR's caution is testimony to the political nature of the system. If complete trust existed between the division and the legislature, the agency would feel less encumbered by such considerations.

While the DWR was tentatively waiting for an opportunity to test the legislative amendments of 1986, other forces were mobilizing to expand that legislation further. Concern among citizens for dewatered streams was not limited to an interest in trout. Instream flow legislation signed in the spring of 1992 can be traced directly to the efforts of a group of citizens living at or near the mouth of Little Cottonwood Canyon because of the loss of the trees. In the mid-1980s, Murray City claimed all of its water rights from Little Cottonwood Creek to operate a power generating plant. The result was to completely dewater the streambed at the mouth of Little Cottonwood Canyon, and the cottonwood trees lining its banks have long since withered and died. This may be a common occurrence at stream segments all over the state, but Murray City's alleged "overuse" angered prominent homeowners in this well-heeled part of Salt Lake County.[59] County commissioners were alerted and the political process of restoring water to Little Cottonwood Creek began. That process is a new chapter in legislating instream flow in Utah.

Legislative History

The legislative history of instream flow reflects a change in the value we place on uses of water. In 1975 a proposal to amend the water code to protect instream flow, which was supported by the governor, failed in two legislative sessions in one year (a regular and a special session).[60] Again in 1983, an instream flow bill failed in committee (H.B. no. 8, 1983, defeated). Legislation enabling the Division of Wildlife Resources to preserve instream flows for fisheries was finally enacted in 1986, but the lobbying did not end with those amendments; many thought the bill was overreaching, while others thought it inadequate.

The high visibility of the drying up of Little Cottonwood Creek, along with the ensuing public outcry, much of which came from a state senator, was the catalyst needed for the expansion of the 1986 amendments that occurred in 1992. In May 1991, the Department of Natural Resources, at the request of Senator Scott Howell, assembled an Instream Flow Task Force comprised of a number of prominent citizens and department heads, chaired by the executive director of the Utah Department of Natural Resources. The Farm Bureau, the Utah Association of Counties, the League of Cities and Towns, the Division of Wildlife Resources, the current state engineer, the Utah Outdoor Alliance, and the Utah Wildlife Leadership Coalition were all represented. Prominent lawyers with reputable backgrounds in water law were also present. Indeed, an impressive number of constituencies were present in this attempt to unite contentious views as to the proper allocation of scarce water.

Senator Howell stated the committee's mission at its first meeting: "to examine existing Utah water law and recommend changes to allow the use of water for the benefit of environmental, ecological, recreational, and other similar values."[61] In striving for conciliation and creativity in the search for common ground, it is to the credit of the chairman, former state engineer Dee Hansen, that so many interests were represented at the table. In a state in which the vested rights of water users have been assumed to be paramount, this task force was the first of its kind to address emerging changes in our water use priorities. Politics can inhibit changes in water law to the detriment of stream flows, but it can also be a productive forum for disparate points of view.

Success of the Task Force

Allocation and distribution of resources through a decision-making body is one way to define politics; the Instream Flow Task Force was a political entity with a political mission. Traditional water users of the state, especially agriculture and industry, were well represented by a lawyer of considerable stature and experience, who argued vehemently against any radical departure from the current scope of the instream flow statutes. Nonconsumptive uses such as aesthetics, recreation, riparian habitat, or anything else that could be codified as a beneficiary of instream flow, constituted such a departure, a "meddling" with vested rights. The group had to decide if its mission was to effect some incremental technical changes in statute wording, such as a modification of the change application statute, or to realize a broader, more substantive change in water allocation. The most serious concern of traditional users, as reflected in this body, was a perceived threat that the state (or the DWR) could invoke the power of eminent domain should instream flow become a dominant use of the flow in a stream. All legislation to date has reflected that uneasiness.

Throughout the meetings, the chair made a concerted effort

to avoid prolonged argument, although philosophical disagreements persisted. Issues that could not be solved in a limited time were deliberately skirted. His dominant strategy was to search out and concentrate on issues where agreement might be found, such as expanding the capacity to acquire instream flow rights beyond the DWR, or eliminating sanctions by the state legislature. He also left the fine tuning of the legislative language to a subcommittee of four lawyers, two representing traditional interests and two who openly advocated change. The chair also attended the intense subcommittee meetings to "referee," and a legislative assistant was present for technical information. Uppermost in the minds of subcommittee members was to hammer out language that would be acceptable to the entire task force before being presented to the interim committee and, ultimately, both bodies of the legislature.

Progress in reaching consensus was made because there was balance among the task force members, allowing for intelligent discussion of the issues. Wildlife and recreational representatives advanced economic arguments, primarily the expanding recreational uses of Utah's streams, to counter those of the vested interests. The central question remained, however, of whether legislation could be amended to award a stream channel segment the legal right to surface water for recreational purposes.

Consensus was eventually reached on the following major point: an instream flow could be recognized as a nonconsumptive use without the presence of a physical diversion, a radical concept in water law in the western states. (Historically, a diversion has been required to obtain a water right; this requirement has been the primary argument of traditional water users to defeat instream flow provisions.) The revised and adopted legislation dispensed with the physical diversion requirement, declaring that "a physical structure or physical diversion from the stream is not required to implement a change for instream flow use."[62] It also granted the Division of Parks and Recreation, along with the DWR, the capacity to purchase water rights for instream flow, although only with funds appropriated by the legislature.[63]

Legislative oversight is unique to Utah and was not advocated by the task force. The prevailing opinion was that the requirement for legislative approval in the 1986 legislation was too restrictive, that a legislative body should not be involved on a day-to-day basis in agency activity, and that it should trust the agency to which it gives statutory authority. The real demand for legislative approval came from the legislature itself, perhaps reflecting a bias toward current water users. This bias, in turn, reflects the concern mentioned earlier that no land or water rights be condemned for purposes of instream flow.

The revisions in the Utah code may not be sweeping, but they are certainly noteworthy. They reflect an increasing awareness of changing economic conditions in the state; they validate the technical feasibility of retaining stream flows in channels; and finally, they recognize a changing administrative and legal climate that may begin to favor instream flow.[64]

The real catalyst for change, however, came from an environmental situation that had turned ugly—the Little Cottonwood dewatering. The advantage was seized by an ambitious legislator as an opportunity to effect change. He also had some critical resources at his disposal in the form of a constituency that was willing and able to mobilize as soon as the appropriate mechanism was established. The Department of Natural Resources was appointed to provide the vehicle for change, and the Instream Flow Task Force was assigned the challenge of finding a remedy. It was headed by a respected and competent official, and the result was an amicable political decision. The hierarchy of water users, virtually all with private economic interests, thus made some room on the ladder for a long-neglected water user with no voice—a stream channel.

Another historic settlement has been reached concerning instream flow on the San Raphael River in Emery County. In November 1994, the Utah Department of Natural Resources, the U.S. Division of Wildlife Resources, PacifiCorp, Emery County water users, and the Bureau of Land Management announced an agreement, several years in the making, that will provide water for wildlife habitat while protecting the water rights of Emery County users and PacifiCorp. When the change application is approved, the DWR will be the recipient of all the irrigation water rights in the San Rafael River below Ferron Creek.

PacifiCorp donated more than 5,000 acres of land along the San Rafael River to the DWR with all water rights in the river, protecting about 80 miles of the San Rafael drainage.

Prior to this agreement, only one small instream flow on the river had been approved. The executive director of the Department of Natural Resources hailed it as a significant action that demonstrates that water can be used to supply instream flows while protecting other uses.[65] PacifiCorp's upstream uses at its Hunter and Huntington power plants are protected by the agreement, and the company acquires an impeccable public image for making a contribution to a desert river that supports significant recreational use. The Department of Natural Resources perceives the transaction as a coup, because "it clearly demonstrates that Utahns can effectively solve difficult water matters without federal intervention."[66]

Conclusion

Acrimonious litigation over water has been a constant feature of western life. The early Mormon bishops spent almost as much time refereeing squabbles over water rights as they did ministering to their wards, especially in rural areas where municipalities were small theocracies.[67] Today the state engineer adjudicates many applications, the more trivial coming from urban residents who request water rights for landscaping, which he cannot acknowledge as a beneficial use because aesthetics is not recognized as a beneficial purpose. Perhaps such requests reveal more about the wealth of Utah's water supply than about its scarcity. Although Utah is, overall, the second driest state in the nation, its system of water allocation mirrors its disparate populations and its varied geography. Instream flow is the latest beneficiary of the water allocation system.

Consequently, the problem is not so much scarcity as an allocation system that is experiencing difficulty meeting the needs of an increasing, and often extravagant, population. Much has been said about the inevitability of conflict as greater numbers of people compete, often with increasing sophistication and political acuity, for an increasing variety of water uses; there is no doubt that there will continue to be conflict. It is also apparent that there can be ample opportunity for innovative solutions. Researchers should begin to focus on the negotiations taking place in many small political arenas. The Division of Wildlife Resources has quietly gone about the business of preserving stream flows, and activity has been taking place regarding the mitigation that is required by the 1992 CUP Completion Act. The agreements arrived at by the Instream Flow Task Force, which were a prelude to the 1992 instream flow amendments, are sufficient testimony to the possibility of greater equity in water allocation.

This is not to say that conflict should be minimized and scarcity ignored. But public policy can become more enlightened. In the past, draconian schemes to conserve water were proposed, including covering bodies of water with a chemical film to retard evaporation, destroying riparian vegetation because of its water consumption, and desalinating marsh water.[68] Such solutions are not politically viable today. The complexity of water management will, however, draw public administrators deeper into disputes. Whether as adjudicators or stakeholders, they will become parties to the disputes pitting streamside residents against consumptive users, irrigators against fishermen, and municipalities against rural populations. The quality of our public debate and the competence of public officials to carefully manage water issues will have a profound effect on Utah water policy.

Notes

1. B. L. Lamb and H. R. Doerksen, "Instream Water Use in the United States—Water Laws and Methods for Determining Instream Flow Requirements," *National Water Summary 1987—Hydrologic Events and Water Supply and Use*, U.S. Geological Survey Water-Supply Paper 2350 (Washington, D.C., 1987), p. 112.

2. J. E. Stromberg and D. T. Patten, "Riparian Vegetation Instream Flow Requirements: A Case Study from a Diverted Stream in the Eastern Sierra Nevada, California, USA," *Environmental Management* 14 (2) (1990): 185–94.

3. Ibid., p. 193.

4. R. Wahl, "Acquisition of Water to Maintain Instream Flows," *Rivers* 1 (3) (July 1990): 196–97.

5. Utah Code Annotated, sec. 73-3-3[11][a][ii].

6. Wahl, "Acquisition of Water," p. 197.

7. Utah Code Annotated, sec. 73-3-3[11][e][i].

8. R. A. Kimsey, "Water Allocation in Utah—Protection of Instream Uses," *Utah Law Review* (Fall 1975): 691.

9. Ibid., p. 691.

10. C. T. DuMars, "Modifying Behavior to Protect Instream Flows," *Rivers* 1 (2)(1990): 160–61.

11. Utah Code Annotated, sec. 73-3-3[11](b).

12. Mark A. Holden, "The Importance of Instream Flow and Recreational Needs in State Water Planning," paper presented at the Sixteenth Annual Conference, Utah Section, American Water Resources Association, Salt Lake City, Utah, April 21, 1988.

13. Ibid., p. 9.

14. R. J. Davis, "Utah Water Rights Transfer Law," *Arizona Law Review* 31 (4)(1989): 841–64.

15. D. H. Getches, *Water Law in a Nutshell* (St. Paul, MN: West Publishing Co., 1990).

16. B. G. Colby, "The Economic Value of Instream Flows—Can Instream Values Compete in the Market for Water Rights?" in *Instream Flow Protection in the West*, ed. by L. J. MacDonnell, T. A. Rice, and S. J. Shupe (Boulder: University of Colorado Law School, 1989), pp. 87–101.

17. Holden, *Importance of Instream Flow*, p. 3.

18. Lori Potter, "The Public's Role in the Acquisition and Enforcement of Instream Flows," in *Instream Flow Protection in the West*, ed. by L. J. MacDonnell, T. A. Rice, and S. J. Shupe (Boulder: University of Colorado Law School, 1989), pp. 41–68.

19. G. A. Gould, "Agriculture, Nonpoint Source Pollution, and Federal Law," *U. C. Davis Law Review* 23 (3)(1990): 461–98.

20. State Water Plan Coordinating Committee, *Utah State Water Plan: Fisheries and Water-related Wildlife* (Salt Lake City,1990) sec. 14.1.

21. Colby, "Economic Value of Instream Flows," pp. 90, 91.

22. Marc Reisner and Sarah Bates, *Overtapped Oasis: Reform or Revolution for Western Water* (Washington, D.C.: Island Press, 1990), p. 109.

23. Ibid.

24. Lamb and Doerksen, "Instream Water Use in the United States," p. 114.

25. Ibid., p. 114.

26. L. J. MacDonnell, "The Water Transfer Process as Management Option for Meeting Changing Water Demands," vol. 1, (Boulder, Colo.: Natural Resources Law Center, University of Colorado report to the U.S. Geological Survey, April 1990), p. 30a.

27. Ibid., p. 29.

28. "Utah Water Rights Transfer Law," p. 863.

29. Ibid., p. 862. This conclusion concerns exchanges and transfers within the state; there are innumerable barriers to water transfers outside the state.

30. MacDonnell, "The Water Transfer Process," p. 30.

31. Utah Code Annotated, sec. 73-3-3[11](ii)(a)(Supp. 1989).

32. W. L. Jackson et al., "An Interdisciplinary Process for Protecting Instream Flows," *Journal of Soil and Water Conservation* 44 (7)(1989): 123.

33. Porter, "The Public's Role," p. 43.

34. Ibid., p. 51.

35. H. C. Dunning, "Instream Flows and the Public Trust," in *Instream Flow Protection in the West*, ed. by L. J. MacDonnell, T. A. Rice, and S. J. Shupe (Boulder: University of Colorado Law School, 1989), pp. 103–35.

36. Kimsey, "Water Allocation in Utah," p. 687.

37. 102 Utah Adv. Rep. 8,9 (1989).

38. 766 P.2d 263 (Nev. 1988).

39. J. W. Steiger, "*Bonham v. Morgan*: Utah's New Criteria for Water Right Change Applications," *Journal of Energy, Natural Resources and Environmental Law* 11 (1)(1990): 143–71.

40. Utah Code Annotated, sec. 73-3-3 [11](1989).

41. Utah Code Annotated, sec. 73-3-8[11](1)(c) (1989).

42. J. W. Steiger, "*Bonham v. Morgan*," p. 166.

43. Ibid., p. 167. NPS can also claim a federal reserved water right to protect the flow of the Virgin River through the park.

44. *Nevada v. Morros*, 766 p.2d 263 [Nev. 1988].

45. L. Potter, "*Nevada v. Morros*: Instream Flow Rights for Nevada," *Rivers* 1 (January 1990): 66.

46. Kimsey, "Water Allocation in Utah," p. 706.

47. Ibid.

48. Jeff Appel (attorney with Haley and Stolebarger, Salt Lake City), interview, November 1990.

49. Robert Morgan (Utah state engineer), interview, December 1990.

50. Wayne Martinson (Audubon Coordinating Council of Utah), interview, November 1990.

51. J. Williams (attorney for PacifiCorp Electric Operations), interview and telephone interview, November 1990.

52. Bob Williams (fish and wildlife biologist, U.S. Bureau of Reclamation, Upper Colorado Region), interview, November 1990.

53. Mark Holden, interview, 1990.

54. Bob Williams, interview.

55. State Water Plan Coordinating Committee, *Utah State Water Plan* (Salt Lake City, 1990).

56. Holden, interview.

57. Ibid.

58. Ibid.

59. "Bangerter Signs In-Stream Flow Bill into Law," *Salt Lake Tribune*, April 6, 1992.

60. D. W. Jensen, "Administrative Strategies for Satisfying Instream Flow Needs," *Proceedings of the Symposium and Specialty Conference on Instream Flow Needs, American Fisheries Society and the American Society of Civil Engineers*, vol. 1 (Boise, Ida., May 1976), pp. 299–314.

61. S. Howell, "Mission Statement," Utah Department of Natural Resources, Instream Flow Task Force (Salt Lake City, May 22, 1991).

62. S.B. no. 7, amending Utah Code Annotated, sec. 73-3-3[11](c).

63. Utah Code Annotated, sec. 73-3-3[11](f)(i).

64. The task force was somewhat concerned about a possible public referendum, which was perceived as "ramming instream flow down our throats."

65. Ted Stewart, "News Release," Department of Natural Resources, November 16, 1994.

66. Ibid.

67. Ted Wilson (mayor of Salt Lake City from 1976 to 1985), interview, April 8, 1991.

68. Kimsey, "Water Allocation in Utah."

PART IV

Conclusions

There was a time when all water policy had a local orientation; if the local people wanted a project, they contacted their congressman and he got them the authorization and the funding for the project. The only "national" element in the entire process was the money—the federal government paid the bill. But today nearly all aspects of water policy are enmeshed in a complex web of interests and claims. This "nationalization" of water policy can clearly be seen in the long struggle to build the CUP. For many years that project was of interest to a handful of Utahns but almost no one else. Now the much-revised CUP is the product of a legislative process that involved senators and representatives from all regions of the country and many facets of water policy, environmental policy, energy policy, taxes, and budgeting. Thus it is impossible to understand contemporary Utah water policy without an understanding of the national context.

In a recent report on water use in the United States, the U.S. Geological Survey noted that the traditional "supply-management" approach to water resources has been supplanted by a new era of "water-demand management." The report identifies a host of reasons for this basic change in policy: "Increasing development costs, capital shortages, government fiscal restraint, diminishing sources of water supply, polluted water, and a growing concern for the environment have forced water managers and planners to begin to rethink traditional approaches to management and experiment with new ones."[1]

In this concluding section, Professor Tim Miller explains how water policy has changed in recent years and relates these changes to the previous chapters in this book. And then to bring the book fully up to date, chapter nine describes the grueling legislative battle that ultimated yielded the 1992 CUP Completion Act, as well as subsequent efforts to implement that law.

Note

1. U.S. Geological Survey, "Estimated Use of Water in the United States in 1990," Circular no. 1081 (Washington, D.C., 1993), p. 2.

CHAPTER EIGHT

Utah Water Politics in a National Perspective

Tim Miller

In the film *The Milagro Beanfield War* there is a compelling combination of themes: angels, magic, and water.[1] The association of these three elements serves as an appropriate introduction to the discussion that follows, which examines Utah's water policy in light of contemporary national and regional trends. While the context is broader, it is not limited solely to matters of federalism or geography; remember that water in western America has a spiritual, larger-than-life quality, related to angels and magic.

Trends in Federal Water Policy

Before considering the particulars of Utah and the West, some stage setting is in order. Essentially, the "traditional approach to the West's limited water resources" at the national level is being stood "on its head."[2] Five major trends are at the heart of Washington's western-states water revisionism: the decline of agriculture and the rise of the new economics, the rise of western cities and the new economics, the success of the environmental movement, the decline of the Bureau of Reclamation, and the decline of the "water status quo."

The Decline of Agriculture and the
Rise of the New Economics

Clearly, the western states form the most arid region of
America. From the southwestern states (the driest of the dry) to
the Rocky Mountain states (with lush valleys scattered around
arid high plains), concern for water has long been fundamental
to life itself. At the outset of the nineteenth century, explorers
and adventurers roamed the region, followed by trappers (1820s
to early 1840s); settlers, soldiers, and prospectors (1840s); and
railroads and more settlers (1860s). For those bent on staying,
finding and capturing water was of paramount concern. This
was particularly true for the region's third wave of economic
activity, the farmers and ranchers who staked claim to the harsh
territory during the last half of the nineteenth century.[3]

Private investors responded to agriculture's needs by establishing privately owned water and storage companies. Soon,
"the federal government . . . stepped in to hasten and encourage
the economic growth and settlement of the West."[4] Spurred on
by increased public awareness of the importance of water—
brought about primarily by the western drought of 1887–90 and
eastern flooding in 1889—Congress responded with increased
U.S. Army Corps of Engineers activity in the East and passage of
the 1902 Reclamation Act. The Reclamation Act "is recognized
as the beginning of many decades of federal involvement in constructing and heavily subsidizing water projects in the West."[5]

With passage of this legislation, the Bureau of Reclamation
soon began constructing federally financed dams and related
projects, thereby "contract[ing] water deliveries with the local
beneficiaries (usually irrigation districts)."[6] Beneficiaries were
"obligated" for reimbursement costs to the federal government,
based on their ability to pay. In effect, however, ability to pay
was a loosely calculated concept that diminished the likelihood
of repayment.

The scope of taxpayer subsidies to agriculture were later
extended to include long-term contracts at little or no interest,
with periods of suspended payments, extension of repayment
periods, and below-cost electric power rates for water pumping.
Eventually, even the 160-acre maximum farm size was aban-

doned. In California's Central Valley Project (CVP), only $50 million, or about 5 percent of the total $931 million spent on the project's irrigation facilities over the last forty years, has been repaid. With an average water price in the late 1980s of $6.15 per acre-foot, the subsidy amounted to more than 90 percent of the actual cost of $72.99 per acre-foot. These subsidies mean large economic rents, or profits, for a relatively small number of people who, predictably, lobby hard to keep them.[7] Although the CVP is merely one project (although a huge one, with annual taxpayer subsidies of $400 million to beneficiaries[8]), it illustrates water subsidy trends across western agriculture.

Enter the "new economic realities" of the late 1980s. Although western agriculture has withstood the assaults of critics for ninety years, it has been increasingly battered, tattered, and torn in light of the new realities Essentially, public opinion is changing with regard to agriculture and these subsidies; in an era of huge public sector deficits and gut-wrenching government prioritizing of services, these subsidies to agriculture are no longer automatically supported by the public. The years of hammering by environmental groups and the recent cycle of drought impacting western cities have taken their toll. But the changing attitudes run deeper. With "three-quarters of the world's available fresh water . . . used for irrigation . . ." and 80 to 90 percent of the available water in the western states earmarked for farmers, many decry not only inequity but waste. Government subsidies, critics charge, invite farmers to waste water through inefficient movement and storage of the precious resource and by squandering it on low-value surplus crops or on crops that are themselves worth less than the water used to produce them.[9]

Large agribusiness interests have likewise been hard hit in recent years, particularly as a result of the public perception that they have abused Bureau of Reclamation policies. In 1982 for example, Congress amended the 1902 legislation, increasing the existing and widely ignored 160-acre limitation to 960 acres for family farms receiving subsidized federal water. But as the *Congressional Quarterly* reported:

> It soon became apparent that even the relaxed definition of a
> family farm was being defied. A 1990 report by the General

Accounting Office noted that the J. G. Boswell agricultural company had evaded the new limits and continued to receive low cost water by placing its 23,000-acre Boston Ranch in California into 326 employee trusts, while retaining control. . . . water meant to go only to small individual farmers has been siphoned off by huge, wealthy corporate farm operators.[10]

Other public perceptions also undermine confidence in large-scale western agriculture. Agribusiness interests are faulted for double dipping, the practice of using subsidized water to grow crops such as rice and cotton, which are in turn subsidized by another federal agency, the Agriculture Department, "cost[ing] taxpayers hundreds of millions of dollars a year."[11] From there, critics charge environmental damage and the declining role of agriculture as a contributor to regional economies. Senator Bill Bradley (D-New Jersey), for instance, calls California "a giant sponge," noting that agriculture uses 85 percent of the state's water while contributing only $20 billion to the state's $760 billion annual economy.[12]

Farm interests counter that their economic contribution is much greater than critics realize and that long-term water contracts (typically for forty years) are necessary for the stability of and continuity in western agriculture and the price of food delivered to consumers. Regardless of the merit of these charges and countercharges, the overall point is that public confidence in western water subsidies for agriculture is no longer universal. The political consequences stemming from this reversal are significant, and farmers are, of course, aware of these changes. In fact, "though resistant, farm interests have recognized the new . . . realities. 'Change is inevitable,' said Jerold Butchert, general manager of the . . . largest irrigation agency in California. . . . The fight is over how far change will go."[13]

The Rise of Western Cities and the New Economics

The second key trend in western water policy stems from the cities. Worldwide populations are shifting from rural to urban areas. By one estimate, "90 percent of population growth in the next forty years will be in cities. As cities grow, and with them industry, their appetite for water will also increase."[14] On at least two fronts, the cities of the American West are not waiting for forty years before expressing themselves on this issue. Western cities are indeed growing rapidly and they are clamoring for more water to support that growth. The implications of these two trends is the "other side of the coin," so to speak, of the decline of agriculture's influence.

With their beauty and numerous amenities, the secret is out: western cities are nice places to live. In fact, "the cities of the West have become some of the fastest growing centers of the world."[15] In many respects this growth is all "well and good" for western cities. But as former Colorado governor Dick Lamm said, speaking literally of Denver but figuratively for all western cities, "Denver is essentially in a no win situation. . . . We've got this dilemma. Where do we get the water to serve those people [who are coming]? . . . Wherever we go, people will be unhappy. I guarantee it."[16] Spurred on by a seven-year western drought in the late 1980s and early 1990s, urban representatives across America began asking why it is that with 90 percent of the population in the West living in cities, 90 percent of available western water goes to agriculture?[17]

The answer to Governor Lamm's question rests with "an odd twist of Reagan-era deregulation, which has made allies of environmental and urban interests in creating a partial free market in water so that it flows to where it has the most value."[18] Or as Lamm suggested in answer to his own question, "Water runs, not downhill, but toward money."[19] Once again, this is the reality of the new economics.

The attempt to quench the thirst of western cities, both existing and anticipated, is taking many forms. From Santa Barbara's desalinization plant and "water cops" who, during the recent extended drought, drove around the city looking for water trails and citing violators, to Denver's effort to tap and pump the San Luis Valley's ocean of groundwater north to the metropolitan area, western cities are becoming increasingly clever and aggressive—some would say ruthless—in pursuing water.

By many accounts the future of western agricultural-urban water relations lies in water transfers. As noted by the assistant general manager of the Metropolitan Water District of Southern

California, "There's a fairly dramatic change taking place—broad support has developed quickly for agricultural water transfers." The California Department of Water Resources, during the height of the 1991 drought, established a "'water bank' that bought water from farmers and resold it to urban users." The process of transferring, or trading, water rights is increasingly common in other western states (such as Colorado), although legal hurdles are also common. And we must recognize the essential point regarding transfers: "slowly, with some reluctance, farmers are beginning to loosen their historic grip on water in the West, transferring some of their supplies to the faster growing cities and industries—for a price."[20]

The second key western water dynamic reshaping federal water policy, then, is the emergence of the cities as independent and increasingly aggressive players in western water politics. In the words of David Behar, executive director of a San Francisco environmental group, "Throughout history, agricultural and urban interests have been in an unholy alliance to insure everybody got what they wanted, at the expense of the environment; that alliance is starting to break down."[21]

Success of the Environmental Movement

Environmentalism has not always been a popular stance. Appeals to environmental aesthetics and morality (passing on a beautiful, clean planet as the morally correct thing to do) were sometimes persuasive, but more often not. No longer do such arguments fall on deaf ears. The third significant pattern redefining the federal approach to western water is the rise of environmental influence, typically traced to the first Earth Day, in 1970, which rallied public attention to environmentalism. The passage of key pieces of legislation during this period—the National Environmental Policy Act, the Endangered Species Act, section 404 of the Clean Water Act, the Federal Land Management and Policy Act, and the Wild and Scenic Rivers Act—enhanced the standing of conservationists and environmentalists in federal court, thereby adding "delay" as a tactic in their arsenal. And frightening scenarios (such as the alleged pending death of Lake Erie or acid rain) and catastrophes (for example, Chernobyl, the *Exxon Valdez*) have increased public consciousness. Thus water specialist Arthur Chan stated in the early 1980s: "The celebration of the Earth Day in 1970 marked a new epoch. An environmentally conscious ethic is being introduced into the American society and culture. A new era is established as a result of the environmental movement. It reflects the changing values in the society since the early 1960s and there is strong evidence that the trend will continue."[22]

Recent polling data suggest that this rise has continued to the present. The Gallup Organization reported in 1991 that "78 percent of Americans consider themselves 'environmentalists.' "[23] Two-thirds of households reported having reduced the use of water, having replaced an inefficient automobile, or avoiding the use of aerosol sprays as aspects of their personal environmental activism. Nearly half (49 percent) of respondents reported they "would specifically avoid buying a product that was not recyclable," and 51 percent "have given money to an environmental cause."[24] The Gallup Organization concludes: "The most obvious achievement of the environmental movement has been the development of a national consensus that acknowledges the seriousness of environmental problems and the public's stated willingness to tackle these problems."[25]

This rise in influence has many sources. None, however, is as central to the movement's successes as one key strategic move: "Environmentalists have become increasingly sophisticated to the point that they are the strongest advocates of economic analysis of federal water resources environmental projects."[26] Accordingly, the environmental movement in recent years has largely downplayed arguments of morality and aesthetics, shifting instead to a strategy of cost containment. As a result, calls for water reuse, marketing, restoration and mitigation, conservation generally, and instream flow, among others, all based on the logic of cost savings, have moved to center stage in federal water policy. Use of the theme of sound economics, "plus a growing national awareness of environmental issues, have given groups like the National Wildlife Federation considerable clout in Congress."[27]

The Decline of the Bureau of Reclamation

From its humble beginnings in 1902 as part of the United States Geological Survey, the Bureau of Reclamation "has grown into a 7,300-employee agency with a $900 million budget and projects in 17 western states." The Interior Department's Bureau of Reclamation first gained fame with the taming of the Colorado River during the 1930s. The project culminated with the "726-foot-high Hoover Dam, which was the largest in the world of its day. Its magnificent engineering enthralled a nation caught up in the Great Depression. . . ." Events of the 1930s touched off a "building frenzy that did not peak until the 1950s" and continued, winding down only slowly, from the late 1970s into the 1980s and 1990s. The decline of the Bureau constitutes the fourth major western water trend with national consequences.[28]

The Bureau approached its structural task with relish. The West was still relatively young and undeveloped; good sites were abundant. So the Bureau built and did so with enthusiasm; after all, it was "set up to build."[29] In time, the Bureau became strongly "committed to structural projects."[30] Norms were established, and the norm of structural response became inculcated into agency culture. As Chan explains: "Consequently, they [Bureau officials] have acquired a certain orientation over the years. When that orientation becomes institutionalized—sometimes by law—members of these organizations will be socialized accordingly. Eventually it is entrenched and cannot be changed readily. Of the two construction agencies, the Bureau is more guilty of this."[31]

During its heyday from the 1940s to the 1960s, the Bureau of Reclamation, backed by a chorus of legislators and interest groups willing and able to benefit themselves and their local economies, emerged as a major player in federal water policymaking.[32] In recent years, however, the Bureau and its prevailing building norm have suffered several setbacks. As prominent water lobbyist Joe Tifanni confided, "Let's face it, the best projects are built."[33] The best projects are typically the least controversial; marginal projects are much more controversial. With increasing controversy, builders are often restrained from building.

The Bureau is also seen as having a "history of mismanagement [and] cost overruns. . . ."[34] Mismanagement and abuse of the system have been charged, as noted earlier, in the Bureau's inability to keep large farm interests from obtaining water intended for small, family-owned farms.[35] A closely related criticism is the widely held view that water development generally, and the Bureau in particular, are the hallmark of pork-barrel politics. In the view of prominent water official Irv Reisler, there has been a deemphasis on water development for just that reason: "The program has a bad reputation, unlike the transportation and health programs, and others. It's viewed as pork, which is a terrible stigma." He explains, of course, that pork-barrel tradeoffs are part of the democratic system. "But people think there's more pork in water than elsewhere. . . ."[36]

Another trend working against the Bureau is the perception that their proagribusiness, builder mentality comes at the expense of environmental considerations and safeguards.[37] Protection of the environment, after all, is historically the mission of other agencies, not the Bureau. Asking builders to reverse "habitual thinking and operational procedures" is an invitation "often met with hostile resistance. To ask a practitioner in a construction agency who is well trained in technical and economic feasibility analyses to consider environmental concerns could be viewed as a threat."[38]

These changes, then, have had two overriding impacts. First, because of the new realities facing them, and with the foremost goal of survival in mind, Bureau officials are changing their prevailing builder norms and culture. In 1987 in fact, "the Bureau declared an end to the days of big water project construction." Instead, "the agency is now struggling to redefine itself as a power, maintenance, and environmental organization."[39] And in late 1993 the Bureau's new director, Daniel Beard, formulated a new mission for the agency that focuses almost exclusively on efficient and environmentally sensitive water management. Thus the Bureau is reconciling itself to its diminished role in the federal water policy arena, at least for the time being.

The Decline of Iron Triangles, Distributive Politics,
and the "Water Status Quo"

Reference was made earlier to "an unholy alliance to ensure
everybody got what they wanted."[40] This is an exaggeration, of
course, but like many exaggerations, there is some truth to it.

As Professor McCool noted in chapter one, federal water
policy-making has long been described as a bastion of distributive politics, functionally operating as "subgovernments" or
"iron triangles." Distributive policies and programs, Randall
Ripley and Grace Franklin explain,

> are aimed at promoting private activities that are said to be desir-
> able to society as a whole. . . . Such policies and programs provide
> subsidies for those private activities and thus convey tangible gov-
> ernmental benefits to individuals, groups, and corporations subsi-
> dized. . . . Decisions about subsidies are typically made with only
> short-run consequences considered. The decisions are not consid-
> ered in light of each other; they are disaggregated. Thus there
> appear to be only winners and no losers.[41]

The key terms here are "subsidies" and "winners." Local
interests want something from the federal government—in this
instance a water project. Farmers, water equipment suppliers,
realtors, bankers, investors, and many others see a variety of
gains from the federal subsidies. Presumably, others support
the project because it is sorely needed and sound. These local
project interests approach local governmental leaders, who in
turn need votes, campaign contributions, and good publicity.
Quick and strong bonds often result. Once united (most likely
only if united), these local interests approach members of their
congressional delegation (who also need local political support
in the form of campaign contributions, endorsements, votes, and
favorable publicity). The local interests, when they are skilled at
the game, concentrate their efforts on the representative and/or
senator from their district or state who has the most favorable
power position. Typically, this means the lawmaker with the
most seniority who serves on the House or Senate committee or
subcommittee with jurisdiction over the relevant subject matter.

By this time, the affected interest groups (for instance, water development associations, organizations representing agriculture, business, financial institutions, labor, etc.) have banded together. They approach (and are most likely welcomed by) the federal government's construction agencies (such as the Army Corps of Engineers, Bureau of Reclamation), who are most anxious to provide their professional services. The key terms here are "subsidies" and "winners." When local interests activate their federal allies on congressional committees, interest groups, and agencies (the "iron triangle"), they each get that they want: jobs, economic activity through "free" federal dollars, favorable publicity for members of Congress, subsidies and influence for interest groups, and opportunities for the builders to build, with political IOUs for all. Whether it is money, influence, or power, all parties obtain subsidies. They are all winners.[42]

That has been the story for over fifty years of federal policy dealing with water, but it is no longer the whole story. For the most part, subgovernment alliances dominate policy-making that is routine, behind the scenes, and "not embroiled in a high degree of controversy."[43] The distributive context of policy-making means that lawmakers take turns bringing the "pork" home to their district or state; Representative Smith supports the project in the district of Representative Jones, knowing that Jones will reciprocate in the future.

For decades this has meant that farm interests, backed by their allies, have basically been able to dominate federal water policy. Then came a series of assaults on the subgovernment norm: public relations campaigns, lawsuits, and political challenges by environmental groups; changing western demographics as urban areas mushroomed; agriculture's decline in economic and political "share"; and the decline in level of support for the mission of the builder agencies. More Americans began to view western water policy as too much pork. Eastern residents asked why they were subsidizing western interests, city dwellers questioned why so much water went to farms rather than cities, recreationists joined conservationists in wondering whether development came at overly steep environmental costs. Accordingly, the behind-the-scenes basis of water subgovernment has been replaced by a contentious and highly visible conflict over basic policy.

As a result, "the political dynamic in Congress has changed.
. . . The two key committees that oversee western water policy
now are no longer the fiefdoms of the Westerners but have siz-
able, eastern blocks."[44]   Although these committees and subcommittees do indeed retain vocal supporters of what are sometimes called the "water buffalo status quo,"[45] they are no longer
the bastions of the unchallenged western water iron triangles
that worked largely behind the scenes.[46]

The decline of the western water iron triangle is the culmination of the four other major trends. In that sense the decline of
the iron triangle is the foremost element of the new reality in
federal water policy. It bespeaks a future vastly different from
the past, and we are midway through the transition; the current
emphasis on balancing the federal budget and eliminating federal programs could further erode the federal water development program. The Republicans who now control the U.S.
Congress are apparently divided on whether to support various
subsidy programs such as western water development and agricultural aid. Truly, the traditional system is being stood on its
head by these new realities.

Utah in Perspective

But what do these changes in federal perspective mean
for Utah? The decline in agriculture noted in the previous section is having a direct impact on rural Utah. A vacuum has been
created by this decline in agriculture and mining, as is evident
in Roy Ramthun's discussion in chapter four. Ramthun notes
that with the decline of Utah agriculture and mining, "tourism is
now the largest industry in . . . Utah." Because towns located
near the state's tourist destinations are growing and thriving,
the appeal of recreation and tourism is obvious.

Ramthun's chapter discusses several interesting policy
developments. First, although it is true that water projects (particularly dams) worldwide often disrupt poor indigenous cultures, this is not a major issue regarding Utah's Jordanelle
Reservoir and State Park.[48] Ramthun carefully notes the great
lengths to which Utah officials went to comply with public noti-
fication and comment requirements. Legal requirements aside,

Utah's obvious enthusiasm in inviting public opinion on the Jordanelle project is reflective of the opening of the water process to broader public input. The people whose views did not prevail may have come away feeling frustrated and perhaps believing they were not truly heard. Nevertheless, the opening of the process at the national level, in the face of the new realities discussed above, is seen in these Utah events as well. This can be interpreted as illustrating the complexities of iron triangle members planning (and subsequently implementing) their strategies at the state and local levels; a problem now exists at the local level that has significant financial and environmental implications. Local leaders are either solidly behind the project or keep their reservations to themselves. Having greater personal stakes in events, the already firm alliance between water conservancy officials, western governors, and developers springs into action for the defense of vested interests. The strategizing is done quietly, behind the scenes, in concert with others having vested interests in the project.

This is essentially the picture drawn by the authors of the preceding chapters when depicting recent events in Utah water policy. Elsewhere I have shown how Utah's defense of the Bonneville Unit of the Central Utah Project against the Carter administration's 1977–78 "hit list" efforts to halt the project was orchestrated by the Central Utah Water Conservancy District leadership, with the governor and his water administrators providing solid support. District officials planned the strategy, coordinated events, and took the lead in the campaign to win public and political support (all based on their expertise and stake in the project). They raised the biggest portion of the campaign funds, kept in constant touch with and guided congressional partners, and generally did what needed to be done.[48] The authors of the present work have confirmed these earlier findings. The discussion in chapter three by Carrie Ulrich and Terry Holzworth clearly illustrates the primacy of District leadership in attempting to "retrofit" the 1958 Water Supply Act to satisfy repayment obligations faced in the 1980s.

In fact, much of the analysis of past water development decisions in Utah can be framed in terms that are consistent with the subgovernment (iron triangle) literature. Ulrich and Holzworth remind us of the vested interests (critics would say "conflicts of interest") present on the district board. Ramthun contends that local politicians and water administrators have the usual reasons (votes, dollars, influence) for supporting almost any water development in Utah. Of course, many of the political mechanisms necessary for this type of policy-making have been in place for many years, as Kurt Vedder demonstrates in chapter two.

The second important point is that the development alliance has traditionally been concerned to keep all pertinent events out of the limelight. This theme invites an array of observations. Overall, the authors of the preceding chapters have shown there is considerable interest in Utah's water issues on the part of affected parties and industries (such as recreation operators with regard to Jordanelle Park), while the public at large remains generally apathetic, although less so than twenty years ago. Evidence cited earlier in this chapter suggests that the rise of the environmental movement and urban influence, together with corresponding declines in the influence of agriculture and the water status quo, have had a significant impact in opening federal water policy-making to broader public scrutiny. The same enhanced emphasis on openness and consensus seeking seems to be taking place in Utah water policy-making.

Although numerous examples of this trend have been seen in Utah in recent years, it all comes down to Don Christiansen's observation that "Broad public involvement from the inception is the key to sound decision making.... "[49] Recognizing that the difficulty in steering the CUP Completion Act through Congress was due to the exclusive nature of the bill, Utah's congressional delegation, and particularly Wayne Owens and Jake Garn, took steps to craft a comprehensive piece of legislation, which was signed by President Bush in October 1992. Instead of a bill narrowly reflecting traditional CUP interests, the new legislation goes much further in preserving fish habitats, overseeing mitigation of environmental damage, regulating the flow of the Provo River, compensating the Northern Ute Indian tribe, shifting construction authority from the Bureau of Reclamation to the District, and raising local cost-sharing levels for future project phases.[50]

This inclusive approach is quite extraordinary. In Utah, at least with regard to recent events, it is as though the behind-the-scenes "engineers" read the handwriting on the wall of the new federal realities and so invited the previously excluded to take part. As one observer put it, "for perhaps the first time in the history of the CUP, Utah's politicians, farmers, environmentalists, and urban interests appear to be on the same side of the issue."[51] It remains to be seen, of course, whether "the CUP legislation (and process of inclusion) is the forerunner of anything or the last of the dinosaurs."[52] It is most likely to be the former.

Elsewhere I have traced the fate of the CUP's public critics during the Carter hit-list period of the late 1970s. With the District leading the way with print and broadcast media campaigns, the Carter people were branded "environmental extremists and kooks." The Salt Lake County attorney and his top assistant, the only prominent public figures to break with the CUP establishment, were openly criticized by prominent members of the Mormon church (which, as noted in previous discussions of Utah history, has been a leading element in Utah's water establishment since before statehood). These attacks were so widespread and vicious that the two officials opted not to run for reelection. Similarly, calls were allegedly made to the president of the University of Utah, suggesting that a university faculty critic of the CUP be fired. In 1983 Utah State University's Water Research Laboratory (WRL) went public with a draft report that included passages viewed by various District leaders as critical of the CUP (especially the section titled "Conflict of Interest Potential"). Although four independent reviewers supported the report's assertions, District officials launched a chorus of charges against WRL personnel as biased, unprofessional, wrong, and improperly entering a subject area where they have no business. When the District's general manager wrote a letter to Utah State University officials threatening to discredit and "oppose future funding from any source to prohibit this type of distorted research by the Utah State Water Research Laboratory," university officials backed off, downgraded controversial wording, and did not publish the document. Such a statement from the head of the politically powerful District (and presumably its allies), directed at an agency that depends

heavily upon the Utah Legislature for funding, was taken in
WRL circles as a threat of major proportions.[53]

Mark Twain tells us that "whiskey is for drinkin' and water
is for fightin'."[54]   In recent years these "battles" in Utah, as the
authors here have shown, have been forming along several
fronts: instream flow, groundwater, conservation, funding, and
jurisdiction. In another context the battle lines are forming
around the prevailing western water myth itself.

There are numerous ways to describe the western water
myth. At the outset of this book, Professor McCool explained
that "The myth of water in western ethos has given rise to a pervasive tendency toward overdramatization." That is obviously
a key ingredient in the myth. Another, McCool claims, is that
water has "become the stuff of legend, endowed with mythic
powers."   And the myth goes even further. The *Congressional
Quarterly* recently reported that there is an ongoing "attack . . .
[on] the traditional notion that a western river is wasted unless
its bounty is spread over farmland or sent crashing through
power-generating turbines."[55]

As Ann Wechsler explains in chapter seven, the politics and
corresponding tensions of instream flow in Utah are in fact
mounting an assault on this long-standing aspect of western
heritage. She also traces the development of the myth, noting
the extent to which traditional factors such as the prior appropriation doctrine, arid climate and scarcity, and growth patterns
in population and industry reinforce the status quo. She goes
further, though, in adding another key element of the myth:
fear. "The value placed on use of water outside the stream
channel is, as a result of this fear of shortages, pervasive in the
state." This view is supported by a traditionally minded "conspiracy of convenience" that has long been successful in playing
the game of the water status quo.

The water battles theme is equally evident in Ann Pole's
assessment of Utah's conservation efforts. Her discussion
depicts Utah as considerably less committed to conservation
than numerous western neighbors (most notably Colorado,
California, and Arizona). In part, this hesitancy can be traced to
fear, because, "Managers in Utah argue that relying on conservation as a new source of supply does not give a 'safe margin'

during times of drought." This resistance in turn stems mainly from Utah's proclivity for water agency profit through the sale of cheap, subsidized water. On this front, then, the realization that Utah has alternatives to large, publicly sponsored storage facilities is politically unpopular and seemingly slow in winning public acceptance beyond lip service. But of course, this too reflects the power of the prevailing water heritage.

Shawn Twitchell's analysis of Utah's groundwater policy in chapter six is also couched in terms of change and competition. His discussion traces recent events regarding both groundwater quality and quantity and focuses on the maneuvering of the broad range of vested interests with stakes in the groundwater issue. The contentiousness associated with groundwater policy-making, he notes, may even be played out as federal-state conflicts over primacy regarding groundwater (particularly in the area of quality control). Such tensions are largely inevitable.

The authors here go further, however, in aiding our understanding of the very difficult realities of jurisdictional boundaries and their bearing, both real and potential, on western water policy-making. Twitchell discusses the vagaries of state and federal disputes over groundwater. There is nothing new, of course, in the realization that the cost and quality of local services (whether water, power, public safety, or education) vary across the boundaries of local governments. The intriguing aspect of the conflicts presented here is an offsetting pattern of economic and political influence. On the one hand, residents of Salt Lake City have an economic advantage concerning the cost of their water in comparison with the price paid by county residents. On the other hand, events surrounding the 1985 CUP election demonstrate the political clout of the county vis-à-vis Salt Lake City. Here we see a municipality willingly yielding a portion of its economic advantage in the interest of broader political realities and the public interest. Once again it appears that in Utah, unending conflict over water is apparently not the only option available to leaders—witness the recent agreement over instream flows for the San Rafael River.

The central theme underlying these chapters, then, is their depiction of varying aspects of the contest for water in Utah. But the theme has one more component: the extent to which political and economic changes forecast the pending redefinition of the western water myth and the beginning of a new era. The conservation movement is showing significant results, as public opinion in the United States and other parts of the world champions a reassessment of the "build as the first and best solution" plank of the myth.[56] Social values, undoubtedly spurred on by the environmental movement's new economic tool, are likewise moving in support of instream flow. Groundwater conflicts today regularly engage urban interests against weakened agricultural interests.[57] And with Utah leading the way, seemingly disparate water interests seem to be increasingly anxious to achieve workable results through consensus-oriented decision making. Truly, these are dynamic times for water policy in western America. The obvious conclusion from these pages is that a redefinition of the western water myth is indeed under way.

There is a link between magic and water in the western water myth. Bill Kurtis explains it by describing what happens when "nonproductive" California desert lands are converted into farmland: "Spill a bit of water on that desert, wave a wand, and something magic happens."[58] The essential ingredient, the source of the magic, is water. Congressman George Miller concurs: "In the 1840s people ran across the country to look for gold nuggets. In the 1940s . . . they figured out that if you put water on the desert, it was as good as gold. These were the alchemists of their time. They understood that if you could get your hands on the water, you could turn it into money."[59]

In the American West, the power of this magic has only increased with time. It is very much in evidence in the chapters of this book. But the present magic of western water is taking many new forms. Rising concern for the environment is beginning to be seen as an economic benefit that, if properly managed, can be used to balance social and cultural costs, while redressing existing inequities. For the myth of water these are interesting times indeed.

Notes

1. *The Milagro Beanfield War*, Universal Pictures, 1988; based on the novel of the same title by John Nichols, 1974.

2. Charles McCoy, "Congress Tilts to West's Cities, Wildlife, away from Farms in Water Policy Bills," *Wall Street Journal*, March 17, 1992, p. A-2.

3. Mohamed El-Ashry and Diana C. Gibbons, eds., *Water and Arid Lands of the Western United States* (New York: Cambridge University Press, 1988), pp. 1–7.

4. Ibid., p. 6.

5. Ibid.

6. Ibid.

7. Ibid., pp. 6–7. Also see E. P. Le Veen, and L. B. King, *Turning Off the Tap on Federal Subsidies* (San Francisco: Natural Resources Defense Council, 1985).

8. McCoy, "Congress Tilts to West's Cities."

9. See "The First Commodity," *The Economist*, March 28, 1992, p. 11; Bill Kurtis (moderator), "Water Wars," *Investigative Reports*, BBC production (summer 1992); Robert Reinhold, "Farmers in West May Sell Something More Valuable Than Any Crop: Water", *New York Times National*, April 6, 1992, p. A-12. In the context used here, "available water" means water that is not set aside for natural resources or that does not flow to the ocean.

10. Phillip Davis, "An Agency in Transition," *Congressional Quarterly Weekly Reports* (March 7, 1992): 530.

11. Ibid.

12. Reinhold, "Farmers in West," p. A-13.

13. Ibid., p. A-12.

14. "The First Commodity," p. 11.

15. Kurtis, "Water Wars."

16. Ibid.

17. Ibid.

18. Reinhold, "Farmers in West," p. A-12.

19. Kurtis, "Water Wars."

20. Reinhold, "Farmers in West," p. A-12.

21. Ibid.

22. Arthur H. Chan, "The Structure of Federal Water Resources Policy Making," *American Journal of Economics and Sociology* 40 (April 1981): 121.

23. A significant number of Utahns also consider themselves environmentalists. Recent polls asked respondents to rate themselves from one to ten, with one indicating no identification with the term "environmentalist" and ten indicating a strong identification with the term; in the last two years between 37 percent and 47 percent of the respondents rated themselves between seven and ten. University of Utah Survey Research Center, "Utah Consumer Survey" (Salt Lake City, January 1994), p. 48.

24. Graham Hueber, "Americans Report High Levels of Environmental Concern, Activity," *Gallup Poll Monthly* (April 1991): 6–12.

25. Andrew Kohut and James Shriver, "Environment Regaining a Foothold on the National Agenda," *Gallup Report* (June 1989): 3.

178 	MILLER

26. David Hampshire, "The CUP Runneth Over," *Utah Holiday* (June 1991): 44.

27. Ibid.

28. Davis, "An Agency in Transition," p. 530.

29. Chan, "The Structure of Federal Water," p. 122.

30. Ibid.

31. Ibid.

32. For an intriguing discussion of the political benefits of bringing a large water project to a member of Congress's home constituents during the building frenzy, see Robert Caro's discussion of Senator Lyndon Johnson's (D-Texas) sponsorship of Marshall Ford Dam (later renamed Mansfield Dam) in *The Years of Lyndon Johnson: The Path to Power* (New York: Alfred A. Knopf, 1982), pp. 369–85.

33. Joe Tifanni (president of the Water Resources Council, 1978-83), interview, July–August 1983.

34. Hampshire, "The CUP Runneth Over," p. 46.

35. Charges of mismanagement, high administrative overhead, and cost overruns resulted in the Bureau being replaced by the Central Utah Water Conservancy District as the builder of the CUP; see chapter two for a discussion of this shift. The change was mandated by the 1992 CUP Completion Act; see chapter nine for a full treatment of the act.

36. Irv Reisler (Linton, Mields, Reisler, and Cottone, Ltd.), interview, July–August 1983.

37. Davis, "An Agency in Transition," p. 529.

38. Chan, "The Structure of Federal Water," p. 123.

39. Davis, "An Agency in Transition," p. 530.

40. See Tim R. Miller, "Recent Trends in Federal Water Resources Management: Are the 'Iron Triangles' in Retreat?" *Policy Studies Review* 5 (November 1985): 400.

41. Randall B. Ripley and Grace A. Franklin, *Congress, the Bureaucracy, and Public Policy*, 4th ed. (Homewood, IL: Dorsey Press, 1987), p. 21.

42. See Daniel McCool, *Command of the Waters: Iron Triangles, Federal Water Development, and Indian Water* (Berkeley: University of California Press, 1987); Ripley and Franklin, *Congress, the Bureaucracy, and Public Policy*, 1987; and Miller, "Recent Trends in Federal Water Resources Management," 1985.

43. Ripley and Franklin, *Congress, the Bureaucracy, and Public Policy*, p. 8.

44. Davis, "An Agency in Transition," p. 527.

45. Hampshire, "The CUP Runneth Over," p. 44.

46. Davis, "An Agency in Transition," p. 527.

47. "The First Commodity," p. 94.

48. See Tim R. Miller, "Identifying and Gauging Policy Subsystems in the Field: An Application," paper presented to the Annual Conference of the Western Political Science Association, San Francisco, March 1988.

49. Sonni Schwinn, "CUP Praises Wasatch County's Public Involvement Program," *Provo Herald*, March 24, 1992.

50. Hampshire, "The CUP Runneth Over," pp. 45–46.

51. Ibid., p. 46.

52. Ibid., p. 45.

53. See Tim R. Miller, "Politics of the Carter Administration's Hit-List Water

Initiative: Assessing the Significance of Subsystems in Water Politics" (Ph.D. diss., University of Utah, 1984), pp. 223 and 248–50.

54. See Patrick G. Marshall, "California: Enough Water for the Future?" *CQ Researcher* (January–December 1991): 222.

55. Davis, "An Agency in Transition," p. 527.

56. See Hueber, "Environmental Concern"; Sandra Postel, *Last Oasis: Facing Water Scarcity* (Washington, D.C.: WorldWatch Institute, 1992).

57. See Kurtis, "Water Wars."

58. Ibid.

59. Ibid.

CHAPTER NINE

Update: The CUP Completion Act of 1992

Daniel McCool

Passing the CUP Completion Act

By late 1987 the CUP was once again running out of money. Congress had increased the authorization for the project on several occasions, but now it was necessary to request another increase. Project sponsors wrote a short bill asking for another $750 million and submitted the bill to Congress. Apparently they expected quick passage, but what they got was four years of acrimonious debate over the fundamental character of western water policy.

In October 1992 President George Bush signed HR 429, a complex omnibus water authorization bill that approved an additional $924.2 million for the CUP and made significant changes in western water policy. Between 1987 and 1992, CUP sponsors, environmentalists, California agribusiness, and practically the entire U.S. House and Senate were involved in a prolonged conflict over the basic philosophy of managing western water. The CUP reauthorization became mired in this struggle; the CUP legislation that emerged in 1992 hardly resembled the simple bill filed four years earlier.

Utah environmentalists had worked in vain to defeat the CUP in the 1985 election, but at the national level environmental groups had considerably more clout. The changes in national water policy discussed by Tim Miller in chapter eight were making things difficult for the CUP. When the reauthorization came before Congress, environmentalists were finally in a position to defeat it. Congressman Wayne Owens (D-Utah) realized this and began redesigning the bill in an effort to gain their support.

After prolonged negotiation, a greatly revised reauthorization bill was submitted that contained numerous environmental mitigation and rehabilitation features. However, these features greatly increased the total cost of the bill, which still included $400 million for the costly irrigation component of the CUP, a very unpopular component among federal lawmakers facing unprecedented budget deficits and over $3 trillion in national debt.[1]

The revised bill developed by Owens attempted to avoid a political stalemate over federal funding by making two critical changes. First, it funded the irrigation component through bonds rather than federal appropriation; these bonds would be repaid by the sale of hydropower. And second, it shifted the funding burden for environmental mitigation measures to public power users, a time-honored strategy. For many years the Bureau of Reclamation had subsidized its irrigation projects with revenues from hydropower, the so-called "paying partner." The Owens bill would generate about $15 million a year from public power users in the Colorado River Basin. Forty environmental and outdoor groups, many of which had fought the CUP for decades, signed up as supporters.[2]

The public power lobby reacted quickly. The Colorado River Energy Distributors Association objected to footing the bill for the proposed environmental mitigation measures. Congressman Howard Nielson (R-Utah) opposed the bill. Again negotiators worked out a compromise designed to appease Nielson, the power companies, and the environmentalists.[3] By then the project had run out of money, so Congress passed a one-year stop-gap funding bill so that work could continue.

Then a new problem arose. The settlement that had been worked out with the Northern Ute Indian Tribe began to unravel. As explained in chapter one, district and federal negotiators had struck a deal with the tribe in 1965 .[4] This 1965 deferral agreement made it possible for CUP construction to continue by relying upon Indian water. Construction of the portions of the project that served non-Indians continued unabated, but the projects promised to the Northern Utes were never built. In the late 1980s another tentative deal was worked out with the tribe, but it failed to yield a final agreement. In 1989 the tribe finally lost its patience. The tribal council rescinded the 1965 agreement and threatened to withhold the tribal waters that were needed by the CUP.[5] Without a Ute settlement, the entire project could collapse. After much negotiation, a new settlement for the Utes was worked out and added to the CUP bill.[6]

By 1990 members of the Utah congressional delegation were once again prepared to fight their way through Congress with a reauthorization bill. By then, however, the situation had become considerably more complicated. The CUP reauthorization bill was included in an omnibus authorization, meaning that numerous projects were combined into one large bill. This is a long-standing strategy designed to maximize the probability of passage by permitting many legislators to add a pet project; the president then must sign the entire bill or veto all of the projects, which inevitably will anger some of his congressional allies. The 1990 omnibus bill quickly grew to massive proportions, with legislators from every western state tossing in a project or two.

By 1990, however, there were many legislators who wanted to dramatically reform western water policy and end the long-standing tradition of federal subsidies for irrigation and other water users. They saw the omnibus water authorization bill as a chance to impose reforms in exchange for the new projects throughout the West. A reclamation reform bill, sponsored by Congressman George Miller of California and passed by Congress in June of 1990, was added to the omnibus bill.[7] This bill mandated two fundamental reforms: it prohibited farms that were larger than 960 acres from receiving subsidized water,[8] and it prohibited farmers from receiving subsidized water if they were growing surplus crops (i.e., collecting double subsidies).[9] These proposals provoked an instant outcry from agribusiness interests that would lose millions in government subsidies if the bill became law.

The 1990 omnibus bill created an unusual political situation.

Many western Republican legislators, especially those from California, vigorously opposed the bill because of the reform provisions. But Utah's Senators Garn and Hatch, also western Republicans, supported the bill because it contained the CUP reauthorization; Utah Congressman Wayne Owens, a Democrat who disagreed with Garn and Hatch on most issues, was a chief sponsor of the bill. Environmentalists, who had fought against such omnibus bills for decades, supported it because of the reform provisions. And the Northern Ute Tribe, which had been at best neglected if not outright cheated by the CUP, testified in favor of the bill because it contained their water settlement. The politics of water had become very, very complicated. An editorial in *U.S. Water News* hailed the bill as "a model" for all other water development programs.[10]

The bill passed in the House, primarily because in addition to policy reforms, twenty-two projects from twenty-two states were included to make it more attractive. In the Senate, however, Senator Pete Wilson of California managed to stop the bill in committee; he was running for governor of California, and the agribusiness giants that would lose some of their government subsidies under the bill were big contributors to his gubernatorial campaign. Wilson subsequently won that race, which removed him from the Senate. And Senator James McClure of Idaho, another vigorous opponent of water reform, retired. With Wilson and McClure gone, the bill's sponsors hoped to have more success in the new Congress.

By 1991 it was becoming much harder to push water bills through Congress, especially if they were perceived as pork barrel. Congress had passed a cost-sharing requirement for all Corps of Engineers projects in 1986; that law did not apply to the Bureau of Reclamation, but the same policy was followed for individual Bureau projects. This meant that the CUP was no longer a big gift from the federal taxpayers; cost-sharing requires local beneficiaries to pay 35 percent of the costs for water development, which could total a maximum of $321.9 million for the CUP. However, this did not dampen the enthusiasm of the bill's sponsors, who introduced the CUP reauthorization again in 1991. By then Senator Bill Bradley of New Jersey had inserted a provision into the omnibus bill to dramatically revise the way the massive Central Valley Project of California finances and allocates water. The conflict intensified.

The CUP's sponsor's had by now been working nonstop for over three years on the bill without success. In frustration Senator Garn declared that he would stop all bills submitted to the Senate Energy and Natural Resources Committee, of which he was a member, until the CUP reauthorization passed. "I'm going to be the Ayatollah, I'm going to take some hostages. Nothing is going to pass the Senate. Don't anybody take me lightly on this."[11]

In the meantime, the project still faced some opposition back in Utah. In 1991 government geologists declared the Jordanelle Dam safe, despite the faultlines in the area; this did not convince some of the people who live downstream from the dam in the Provo River Valley. Opposition to the project also arose in the Uinta Basin. In the early drafts of the bill, two dams were to be built for that basin, but both of them were excluded from subsequent versions because of environmental consequences and the lack of feasible dam sites. CUP sponsors countered this opposition by adding to the reauthorization a "Uinta Basin Replacement Project" that allocates $30.5 million for projects in the basin. Trouble also arose in the Heber area. A county commissioner characterized the revised CUP bill as a "rape of Wasatch County" because it would divert water currently used for irrigation in that area.[12] In late 1991 Congressman Bill Orton worked out a compromise by inserting into the bill $30 million in funding to replace that water.[13] In short, CUP sponsors continued the age-old strategy of converting project opponents into supporters by adding them to the list of project beneficiaries.

By late 1992 the omnibus bill had been through so many revisions that legislators found themselves considering the "Senate Amendment to the House Amendment to the Senate Amendment." *CQ Weekly Report* noted that the bill "started life as the popular biennial reauthorization of the Bureau of Reclamation's dam-and-irrigation-construction program. But its popularity attracted pork, and the bill has now bloated to 40 titles."[14] Congressman Wayne Owens continued in his role as legislative coordinator for the CUP provisions in the bill. Both houses passed different bills; the Senate version lacked the reforms for the Central Valley Project in California, which made the bill unacceptable to Congressman Miller, chairman of the House Interior and Insular Affairs Committee. When the bill was considered by a House-Senate conference committee, sixty-one legislators were on hand to protect their part of the bill. Despite a last-ditch effort to stop the bill by Senator John Seymour of California, the conferees agreed on a bill that contained the requested money for the CUP and significant reforms in western policy. However, California agribusiness was successful in stopping the provision in the bill to halt double subsidies and to circumvent the 960-acre limit. Thus the bill contained some, but not all, of the proposed reforms, and plenty of money and projects for nearly all interested parties. The bill passed Congress on October 8, 1992. Senator Jake Garn declared, "We have exhausted ourselves to forge a consensus."[15]

It was not at all clear that President Bush would sign the omnibus bill, however. Both parties in the Congress had supported the bill because it contained projects for just about everyone, but most of the powerful California delegation had opposed it due to the reforms imposed on the Central Valley Project. Bush's secretaries of interior and agriculture, both sensitive to the interests of California agribusiness, advised a veto. President Bush, in a desperate bid for reelection, had to consider how a veto would impact the California vote. It seemed that after four years of wrangling, the CUP Completion Act might die becouse of presidential politicking.

The *Salt Lake Tribune* editorialized: "President Bush will betray the West's voters if he vetoes funds for water projects."[16] The Central Utah Water Conservancy District convinced the *Orem-Geneva Times*, the *Provo Daily Herald*, and *Deseret News* to publish the phone number of the White House so that Utahns could call President Bush. At the last possible minute, Bush signed the bill.

Title II (there are fifty titles in the act) of the 1992 Omnibus water authorization act authorizes $924,206,000 for completing the Central Utah Project, including $242.5 million for the Bonneville Unit.[17] Congressman Owens noted that the CUP Completion Act was unique in that it authorized money for a

big water project but also focused on conservation and environmental concerns: "Not only does it provide 60 years of water
for Salt Lake and Utah counties, it does more for fishing and
wildlife than previous legislation. It is the most environmentally sensitive of any water project to pass Congress."[18] To
Don Christiansen, the District's general manager, the CUP
Completion Act was "the beginning of a new era" in federal
water policy.[19]

The provisions of the act can be divided into four categories:
funding for construction; management and financing reforms;
recreation, conservation, and wildlife measures; and the
Northern Ute Indian Tribe water settlement.

Funding for Construction

The CUP act begins by deauthorizing eight features of the
project, including the dikes in Utah Lake and the Mosida pumping plant. These features had become a political liability for the
project, due to cost considerations and environmental impact;
the new law prohibits using any of the authorized funding for
their construction. The law also includes a sunset provision that
gives the state of Utah and the U.S. Congress five years to
appropriate the necessary funding for the project. The funds
allocated to specific features of the project include:

$150 million for the irrigation and drainage portion of the
Bonneville Unit. This feature of the project engendered a
great deal of opposition, because of its high cost and heavy
subsidies to farmers. To ensure a demand, the law requires
that 90 percent of the irrigation water must be under binding
contract before construction begins.

$10 million for the "water efficiency project" in Wasatch
County and an additional $500,000 for a study of water effi-
ciency. This is part of the deal worked out by Congressman
Bill Orton.

$69 million for the Diamond Fork system. This feature
transports water from Strawberry Reservoir to the Spanish
Fork River.

$30,538,000 for the Uinta Basin Replacement Project. This
is a series of small dams and canals that are "more economi-

cally and technically feasible and more environmentally desirable" than the two large dams originally planned by the Bureau.[20] Many environmental and outdoor groups criticized the dams in the original CUP plan because of their negative impact on fish habitat.[21] The District claims that these new dams in the Uinta Basin provide "stream fishery enhancement opportunities."[22] This section of the bill also provides funds to rehabilitate the Uintah Indian Irrigation Project, which was originally designed to serve Indians on the Uintah and Ouray Indian Reservation; now approximately one-third of the project's assessable acreage belongs to non-Indians.

Management and Financing Reforms

The CUP Completion Act made several significant changes in the way the CUP will be funded and operated:

It took the project away from the Bureau of Reclamation and made the District the primary program manager. The District may select the construction agent for the project, and it has the option of selecting the Bureau of Reclamation if it so desires. This change in project management was in response to criticisms that the Bureau had wasted money on unnecessary administrative overhead and cost overruns and was unresponsive to local input. The District, however, had experienced its own management problems.[23] To maintain federal oversight, the U.S. comptroller general will conduct an audit of the project within one year of its completion.

The act provides funding for numerous studies to increase the efficiency of water usage in the project area, including $10 million for a study of the conjunctive use of surface and groundwater; $1 million for a Utah Lake salinity control study; $2 million for a study of the Provo River, including a study of the feasibility of the Wallsburg Tunnel. This tunnel would deliver water from Strawberry Reservoir to Deer Creek, which means that the water currently scheduled to go to farmers in the Sevier River area could instead be used as municipal and industrial water in the Salt Lake Valley. Proponents of the tunnel argue that this would make more economic sense.

The act requires a nonfederal cost share of 35 percent, which totals $321,870,000 if all identified features are constructed. This money must be provided annually as planning, design, and construction progress.

The District must complete a "definite plan report" for the Bonneville Unit. One of the purposes of such a plan is to ensure that the project follows all applicable federal environmental statutes.

The counties in the District service area (except Salt Lake and Utah) may elect to receive a rebate of the taxes they have paid into the project already, in lieu of irrigation water.

The District must prepare a "water management improvement plan," with the goal of increasing efficiency so that 30,000 acre-feet can be saved through conservation and efficiency measures. A "water conservation pricing study" must be included in the plan. The purpose of the study is to investigate how pricing affects demands. The plan must also include a study of "cost-effective flexible operating procedures."

The act allocates $53 million for conducting these studies and plans.

The act requests that the governor establish a "Utah Water Conservation Advisory Board" that will recommend water conservation standards.

The act prohibits diversion of water out of the Colorado River Basin for the sole purpose of generating hydropower. Also, the secretary of interior is authorized to levy a "surplus crop production charge" on any water used to grow crops that are already in surplus. These two provisions were inserted to meet national political objectives and were necessary to gain the support of legislators from other states.

Recreation, Conservation, and Wildlife Measures

The conservation and fish and wildlife provisions in the act were part of the concessions made to outdoor and environmental groups in exchange for their support of the CUP. Title III establishes a "Utah Reclamation Mitigation and Conservation Commission," with a long list of duties in order to coordinate the mitigation and conservation measures required by the statute. Title IV creates a "Utah Mitigation and Conservation Account" to pay for such activities. The rationale for this account is presented in section 401: "the state of Utah is one of the most ecologically significant States in the Nation, and it is therefore important to protect, mitigate, and enhance sensitive species and ecosystems through effective long term mitigation." The account will be funded from 1994 to 2001 through an annual $3 million "voluntary contribution" from the state, $5 million annually from the federal government, $5 million annually from the Western Area Power Administration, and $750,000 annually from the District.

Northern Ute Indian Water Rights Settlement

Title V of the CUP Completion Act is an attempt to compensate the Northern Ute Tribe for the loss of benefits that would have accrued if the projects promised in the 1965 deferral agreement had been built. The tribe will receive a portion of the proceeds from the sale of Bonneville Unit water used for municipal and industrial purposes. The settlement also authorizes $45 million for tribal farming and a feedlot, a $125 million trust fund for tribal economic development, and funds for stream, reservoir, and habitat improvement. Additionally, $10 million will be used to help the tribe improve its hunting and fishing. In return for these benefits, the tribe permits the CUP to use some of its water and waives all claims arising out of the 1965 deferral agreement.

Implementing the CUP Completion Act

With the passage of the completion act, it appeared that Utah would finally get to finish the project it began a generation ago. But passage of such a law is at the same time the culmination of one struggle and the beginning of another. Several challenges lie ahead.

First of all, the District must come up with enough money to cover the nonfederal cost share. The total amount of this cost share would be $321.9 million if the entire project is built; however, some aspects of the project, such as the I&D component, have been scaled back, which will reduce the total amount to be paid.[24] Don Christiansen, the District's general manager, estimates that the cost share may eventually be pared down to close to $100 million.[25] The District has identified five possible revenue sources to generate increased tax revenue for the cost share:[26] municipal bonds issued by the district or the state; a "small tax" added to water bills; "environmental rehabilitation funds," from designated tax revenue; the sale of water and hydropower to "out-of-state entities"; and appropriation by the state legislature.

A plan proposed by the District to the 1993 session of the state legislature would have doubled the property taxes levied by the District.[27] The District must get approval from the legislature to raise its maximum allowable tax rate; it already collects the maximum taxes permitted under existing law.[28] A deal worked out in the last days of the 1993 legislative session delayed the need for a tax increase for one year. The following year, Governor Mike Leavitt, reminded of his campaign pledge to avoid any tax increases, vowed not to seek any new revenues in the 1994 legislative session for the CUP.[29] A task force appointed by Governor Leavitt that year developed a plan that minimizes the state's contribution for the next two years. This permitted the Utah Legislature in 1994 and 1995 to avoid having to consider the question of raising taxes to pay for the CUP, putting off the difficult task of raising the capital at least for two years. After that, the task force noted that new sources of revenue must be identified, suggesting the following sources: "a broad-based water franchise fee on retail water sales, a surcharge on CUP water, recapitalization of the state's water loan portfolio, development impact fees, recreation fees, environmental mitigation fund revenues, additional property taxes, and future power development revenues."[30] As one state legislator said in the 1994 session, "sooner or later the piper will have to be paid or we don't finish the CUP."[31]

There is some question as to whether the taxpayers of Utah are willing to bear this additional tax burden. A recent poll of the twelve-county area of the Central Utah Water Conservancy District found that residents are opposed to increases in water rates.[32] The state budget is perceived as already overcommitted, and property taxes are perceived as too high; every new expenditure must necessarily be balanced by a reduction in expenditures for other purposes. Thus taxpayers must choose: Do they want more water for their bluegrass lawns or better education for their children? Do they want to subsidize hay farmers in Utah and Juab counties or improve the state's transportation infrastructure? Do they want more fish and wildlife habitat or a better criminal justice system? Lieutenant Governor Olene Walker recently alluded to the zero-sum nature of this decision: "We've got to use some common sense. It's hard to justify (the cost) for raising alfalfa."[33]

The District and its allies argue that it would be senseless to stop funding the project, now that over a billion dollars have already been spent. They also argue that the cost share is a lever to bring in millions of dollars of federal funds; a 1993 District publication states, "In effect, the state leveraged $179 million [in local taxes] to receive $922 million [from federal taxes]."[34] In addition, the District has delineated the benefits that can be purchased with this money: it claims that the CUP Completion Act will produce 7,100 new jobs in construction; an expenditure of $3.4 million per year in operation and maintenance costs; an increase in farm income of $40 million per year; expenditures of $270 million per year for recreation, fish, and wildlife; and an increase in property values of $6 billion.[35]

Even if the state and the District come up with the increased taxes for the cost share, there is no guarantee that Congress will actually appropriate the funding authorized in the Completion Act. A project "authorization" merely gives Congress permission to allocate funding for that project in one of the annual appropriation bills; each year project supporters must compete for money with other federally funded programs. And like the state budget, the federal budget is also a zero-sum situation, meaning that an appropriation for one purpose usually means that a like amount must be cut from some other program. Given the current emphasis on cutting the federal deficit, which totaled $203 billion in fiscal year 1994, it will probably be increasingly difficult to secure funding for multibillion-dollar water projects.

A second threat to the CUP Completion Act is the continuing

conflict with the Northern Ute Tribe. The Ute water settlement in the bill was accompanied by a "Ute Indian Compact" between the state of Utah and the tribe. Both the tribe and the state legislature must ratify that compact before it can be implemented; at this writing, the tribe has not scheduled a referendum to vote on the compact, and the state legislature will not vote on the compact until after the tribal referendum. In the meantime the tribe has claimed it must be remunerated for CUP diversions of its water; in January 1994 the tribe sent a bill to the District for $33 million, for the "unauthorized diversion" of tribal water "pending resolution of the tribe's water rights claims."[36]

A third problem in implementing the Completion Act is the continuing need to keep the tenuous coalition together. Environmentalists, farmers, and developers often clash. The District has made much of the support the project has received from environmentalists, but this support came at a price, and some project supporters are now balking at paying that price. In February 1993 the District's governing board refused to renew three contracts for environmental studies. Board member Tom Hatch said that it was unfair to "buy them off."[37] The board later reversed itself, but cracks in the coalition were beginning to show.

Another conflict between environmentalists and farmers involves different interpretations of water conservation. The Completion Act requires the District to fund conservation projects; since 1993 the District has received over twenty-five proposals for spending the money set aside for water conservation. The District chose to fund three farm proposals that enabled farmers to switch from wasteful flood irrigation to sprinkler irrigation systems. However, these proposals did not offer to use the saved water for public benefits or environmental mitigation; rather, the farmers simply wanted to use the saved water to grow another crop of alfalfa. Environmentalists cried foul, arguing that a public investment in these private lands should result in a public use of the saved water. The District funded them anyway.

A fourth threat to the CUP emerged in early 1993 when

farmers in the Sevier River region asked local counties to withdraw from the Central Utah Water Conservancy District's twelve-county coalition. In July of 1993 Millard County residents in fact voted to withdraw from the project. Voters in Sevier County followed suit in September. Initially the District voiced strong opposition to allowing the counties to withdraw. However, after more than a year of negotiations, the District agreed to formally deannex the two counties and return part of the funds they had paid. This means that Millard and Sevier counties are no longer part of the District or the CUP. Sanpete and Piute counties are now also considering leaving the District and the project.

Since the passage of the CUP Completion Act, the District has attempted to address such problems with a management approach that stresses public participation and openness. A recent District publication states that "The guiding principle of the CUWCD is based on public participation. The District urges every Utahn to make suggestions and ask questions as Utah's future is at stake."[38] As a federal agency, the District must comply with the public participation provisions of the National Environmental Policy Act and other federal laws. It has held a series of scoping meetings, public hearings, and comment periods for all of its activities. Without a doubt, the District is more open than ever before.

In addition to public participation, the District is conducting a well-funded publicity campaign, complete with full-color tabloids in local newspapers and a free videotape that is "part of the District's public information program."[39] The video features a local television news anchorman in a simulated newscast that sings the praises of the CUP (but does not specify the costs). A recent newspaper advertisement by the District features a photograph of a father bathing an infant under the headline: "Dam. We're Good."[40]

The 1992 CUP Completion Act was the end of one political battle and clearly the beginning of another. In the next few years the citizens of Utah and their elected leaders will have to make some very important decisions regarding the use of water and how they want to pay for it. Ted Stewart, the director of the

Utah Department of Natural Resources, recently estimated that the state will spend $2 billion on water development in the next ten years.[41] Raising the money will be quite a challenge.

Current approaches to water policy reflect a mixture of both new and old thinking. In terms of new thinking, Utah water leaders have recently been discussing the possibility of leasing water to other states downriver on the Colorado; such a thought would have been considered heresy just five or ten years ago.[42] But the old water myths die hard. The assumption that water is the deciding variable in all things—the hydrological determinism discussed in chapter one—lives on. At a "Utah Water Summit" held in November 1994, "participants were urged to support efforts to help secure dollars for water to ensure continued economic growth in the state."[43] There is still a widely held belief in the American West that the economy will bloom as the rose if only we can get more water. The reality is, of course and unfortunately, much more complicated than that.

This book has discussed many facets of water in Utah. Perhaps the simplest lesson we can learn from this book is that Utah's water policy has ranged from pork barrel to profound. As to the former category, all Utahns need to take a serious look at how we are spending the public's money for water development. In the latter category, however, there is much of which we can be proud. When the pioneers of Salt Lake Valley first diverted City Creek, they took the first step toward protecting the people's water supply; the system they established still serves us well today. Each time we take a drink of water, we should thank them.

Notes

1. *Salt Lake Tribune,* April 2, 1988, p. B-1.

2. *Salt Lake Tribune,* June 15, 1988, p. B-4.

3. *Salt Lake Tribune,* July 29, 1988, p. B-6.

4. Central Utah Water Conservancy District, Deferral Agreement, Contract no. 14-06-W-194 (September 20, 1965).

5. Tribal Resolution no. 89-175 (September 20, 1989). See Daniel McCool, "The Northern Utes' Long Water Ordeal," *High Country News,* July 15, 1991: 8–9.

6. This settlement was accompanied by a compact between the tribe and the state of Utah; at this writing the tribe has not yet ratified the compact.

7. HR 2567, 101st Congress, 2d. sess., 1990.

8. The original 1902 Reclamation Act stipulated that farms of up to 160 acres could receive subsidized water from federal reclamation projects. In 1982 the acreage limitation was increased to 960 acres, but many agribusiness companies developed surreptitious ways to circumvent this limitation. Congressman Miller's amendment was designed to stop that practice; ultimately, however, this effort failed.

9. The federal government helps farmers by reducing the market supply of crops that are so abundant that the price falls below an acceptable minimum. When the Department of Agriculture declares a specific crop to be in surplus, the government provides a variety of subsidies and incentives to reduce the supply of that crop. Miller argued that it made no sense to have one federal policy that discourages production of a surplus crop and another federal policy that encourages production of the same crop by offering water subsidies. This proposed reform was also ultimately omitted from the final legislation.

10. *U.S. Water News*, November, 1990: 6.

11. *Salt Lake Tribune*, November 21, 1991, p. A-1.

12. *Wasatch Wave*, December 10, 1991, p. A-6.

13. *Wasatch Wave*, July 29, 1992, p. 1-A. Farmers using Daniels Creek water were provided with a $7 million replacement source of water. Thus the cost of the water far exceeds the value of the land being irrigated. See Tom Melling, "The CUP Holds the Solution: Utah's Hybrid Alternative to Water Markets," *Journal of Energy, Natural Resources, and Environmental Law* 13 (1993): 176.

14. *CQ Weekly Report* (October 5, 1992): 2626.

15. Quoted in an information packet distributed by the District titled "Progress Report: Central Utah Water Conservancy District Accomplishments Prior to Enactment of H.R. 429" (n.d.).

16. *Salt Lake Tribune*, October 22, 1992, p. A-22.

17. The act is officially known as the 1992 Reclamation Projects Authorization and Adjustment Act, P.L. 102-575, signed October 30, 1992.

18. *Deseret News*, October 8, 1992, p. A-2. For an excellent description of the act and the political process that lead to its passage, see two articles by Tom Melling: "The CUP Holds the Solution: Utah's Hybrid Alternative to Water Markets," *Journal of Energy, Natural Resources and Environmental Law* 13 (1993): 159–207; and "Dispute Resolution within Legislative Institutions," *Stanford Law Review* (July 1994): 1101–39.

19. Interview with Don Christiansen, general manager, Central Utah Water Conservancy District, March 15, 1995.

20. Central Utah Water Conservancy District, "CUP Completion Act UBRP Scoping Summary," BO0110011BE9.WP5/mm (Salt Lake City, 1993), p. 1.

21. At one point the Bureau of Reclamation proposed to divert most of the water from Rock Creek and then pump the little remaining water in the stream back up the mountainside so it could again run down the streambed and thereby increase instream flows. The Bureau later abandoned this scheme and agreed to a guaranteed minimum flow to protect fish habitat.

22. Quotation from an information packet distributed by the District titled "Progress Report: Central Utah Water Conservancy District Accomplishments Prior to Enactment of H.R. 429, information sheet on the Uintah Basin Replacement Project" (Orem, Utah, n.d.).

23. Office of the Legislative Auditor General, "A Performance Audit of the Central Utah Water Conservancy District," Report no. 89-12 (Salt Lake City, December 1989). It should be noted that most of the problems identified in the 1989 performance audit have been rectified; see chapter three.

24. The original I&D project has been replaced by a much smaller project named the Spanish Fork/Nephi Supplemental Irrigation Delivery System.

25. Interview, March 15, 1995.

26. These five sources were listed in a tabloid insert that appeared in local Sunday newspapers on February 13, 1993, titled "Just Add Water Wisely," prepared by the Central Utah Water Conservancy District.

27. Based on a proposed increase from .0004 to .001. The district taxes on a $100,000 home would therefore rise from $27 to $68. See *Salt Lake Tribune*, February 10, 1993.

28. The district currently collects about $14 million a year from property taxes and water sales.

29. "Leavitt Won't Support Any Tax Increases at Legislative Session," *Salt Lake Tribune*, November 25, 1993, p. C-1.

30. Central Utah Project Funding Task Force, "Final Recommendation to Governor Michael O. Leavitt" (Salt Lake City, December 6, 1993), p. 4.

31. *Salt Lake Tribune*, January 16, 1994, p. B-5.

32. Poll conducted by Dan Jones and Associates, commissioned by the Water Management Improvement Studies Office of the Central Utah Water Conservancy District (Salt Lake City, August 1993).

33. *Salt Lake Tribune*, November 8, 1992, p. 6-D.

34. CUWCD, "Just Add Water Wisely."

35. CUWCD, "CUP," photocopy (Salt Lake City, January 1993).

36. See Daniel McCool, "Utah and the Ute Tribe Are at War," *High Country News*, June 27, 1994, p. 12.

37. *Deseret News*, March 25, 1993, p. B-1.

38. CUWCD, "The Central Utah Project Completion Act," color brochure (n.p., n.d.).

39. Ibid.

40. *Salt Lake Tribune*, August 14, 1994, p. A-10.

41. State Water Development Commission, minutes, October 18, 1994, p. 3.

42. "Leasing Water May Help Utah Cash Flow," *Salt Lake Tribune*, November 11, 1994, p. A-1.

43. Utah Division of Water Resources, *Utah Water Education and Conservation*, newsletter (January 1995): 2.

Index